the **center** for
hermeneutical studies

in HELLENISTIC and MODERN CULTURE

The GRADUATE THEOLOGICAL UNION & The UNIVERSITY of CALIFORNIA
BERKELEY, CALIFORNIA

colloquy

42

EDITOR:

Executive Committee 1981/82:

Julian C. Boyd

Mary Ann Donovan

Victor R. Gold

Erich S. Gruen

Irene Lawrence

Charles E. Murgia

Wilhelm Wuellner
   (Chairman)

The [...] for hermeneutical [...] took its [...] to a
growing awareness [...] humanistic
research, speci[...]ical
Judaica, and st[...]

In [...] growth
in these fields, [...] ly
occur where scho[...] iously
in pursuit of co[...] the
Graduate Theolog[...]
Studies in Helle[...] and modern culture, during the Spring of 1969. The
next step was the creation of a network of relationships and cooperation
between scholars of the Graduate Theological Union and those in various
fields within the University of California who share their interests in
Hellenistic studies and in the problems of hermeneutics involved in their
significance for modern culture.

The Center brings together faculty members of the departments
of Classics, Comparative Literature, English, Folklore, History, Law, Near
Eastern Studies, Rhetoric, and others at the University of California, and
from the Graduate Theological Union including the Center for Judaic Studies,
as well as select graduate students from each institution, and from other
universities and research institutes.

Besides monthly or quarterly colloquies, published in the Protocol
Series of the Center, the Executive Committee of the Center organizes and
schedules Task Force Work Projects and Research Seminars.

the CENTER for HERMENEUTICAL STUDIES

in HELLENISTIC and MODERN CULTURE

The GRADUATE THEOLOGICAL UNION & The UNIVERSITY of CALIFORNIA
BERKELEY, CALIFORNIA

PROTOCOL OF THE FORTY-SECOND COLLOQUY: 14 MARCH 1982

THE PROBLEM OF MIRACULOUS FEEDINGS IN THE GRAECO-ROMAN WORLD

ROBERT M. GRANT
CARL DARLING BUCK PROFESSOR OF HUMANITIES
PROFESSOR OF NEW TESTAMENT AND EARLY CHRISTIANITY
UNIVERSITY OF CHICAGO DIVINITY SCHOOL

IRENE LAWRENCE, *Editor*

Copyright © 1982 by CENTER FOR HERMENEUTICAL STUDIES

All rights reserved

ISSN 0098-0900

Key title:
Protocol of the colloquy of the Center for Hermeneutical Studies in Hellenistic and Modern Culture

Library of Congress Cataloging in Publication Data
Main entry under title:

The problem of miraculous feedings in the Graeco-Roman world.

(Colloquy, ISSN 0098-0900 ; 42)
Bibliography: p.
1. Miracles—Congresses. 2. Food—Religious aspects—Congresses. I. Grant, Robert McQueen, 1917- .
II. Lawrence, Irene, 1942- . III. Series: Colloquy (Center for Hermeneutical Studies in Hellenistic and Modern Culture) ; 42.
BL487.P76 1982   291   82-9676
ISBN 0-89242-041-3

Published by

The CENTER FOR HERMENEUTICAL STUDIES in
Hellenistic and Modern Culture

2465 Le Conte Avenue
Berkeley, CA   94709
USA

TABLE OF CONTENTS

Robert M. Grant
THE PROBLEM OF MIRACULOUS FEEDINGS IN THE GRAECO-ROMAN WORLD   1-15

RESPONSES

Peter Brown, *Professor of History and Classics*   16-24
University of California, Berkeley

K. M. Irwin, *Ph.D. Student*   25-27
Graduate Theological Union

Irene Lawrence, *Lecturer in Religious Studies*   28-31
University of California, Davis

Mary Rosenthal Lefkowitz, *Andrew W. Mellon Professor in Human-*   32-33
Wellesley College   *ities*

Susan Marie Praeder, *Assistant Professor of Theology*   34-37
Boston College

MINUTES OF THE COLLOQUY

List of Participants   38

The Discussion   39-51

SELECT BIBLIOGRAPHY OF ROBERT M. GRANT   52

THE PROBLEM OF MIRACULOUS FEEDINGS IN THE GRAECO-ROMAN PERIOD

ROBERT M. GRANT

A conspicuous feature of the four gospels is the presence of what used to be called "nature miracles." These provided considerable embarrassment to enlightened Christians arguing with critics like Porphyry or with Christian adherents of literal exegesis. Modern critics have sometimes lumped them together and treated them as "Hellenistic" intrusions which corrupted the purely philanthropic/medical story of the Jesus who "went about doing good and healing all who were oppressed by the devil" (Acts 10:38). The miracles of feeding, of the multiplication of bread and wine, and of miraculous fertility seem to constitute a special class, however, not identical with the kind of miracles in which walking on the surface of water or ascending into the sky are in view. We shall consider the role they have played in (1) apocalyptic eschatology, (2) analysis of past and present, (3) relation to possible pagan frameworks, and (4) relation to ideas of providential care and the gospel of work. A subsidiary question, almost always latent, has to do with the credibility of the promises and the nature of their exegesis, whether literal or not.

Visitors to Palestine are usually struck by the omnipresence of the desert in the vicinity of the Promised Land, and they can see what the prophets meant when they spoke of water and crops. Isaiah, for example, spoke of a real land when he wrote, "The wilderness and the dry land shall be glad, the desert shall rejoice and blossom" (35:1). Or Ezekiel (47:7-12):

> This river [from beneath the temple] flows toward the eastern region and goes down into the Arabah; and when it enters the stagnant waters of the [Dead] sea, the water will become fresh. And wherever the river goes every living creature which swarms will live, and there will be very many fish.... And on the banks, on both sides of the river, there will grow all kinds of trees for food. Their leaves will not wither nor their fruit fall, but they will bear fresh fruit every month, because the water flows from the sanctuary. Their fruit will be for food, and their leaves for healing.

Toward the end of the Apocalypse of John (22:1-2) this becomes "the river of the water of life, bright as crystal, flowing from the throne of God and of the Lamb[1] through the middle of the street of the city; also, on either side of the river, the tree of life [Gen. 2:9] with its twelve kinds of fruit, yielding its fruit each month; and the leaves of the tree were for the healing of the nations." The holy city will come down from heaven, even though it will be on earth. In the Epistle of Barnabas (11:10-11) baptismal spirituality

---

[1] The water issues thence because there will be no temple (Rev. 21:22).

is applied to Ezekiel. The river is the water of baptism; we are the trees; eating the fruit means hearing and believing.

Perhaps a similar tendency can be detected in the promises of Matthew 5:6 as compared with Luke 6:21. Luke contrasts being hungry now with being filled in the future. (There is also a "woe" upon those who are full now; they will be hungry later, 6:25.) Matthew, on the other hand, speaks of those who "hunger and thirst for righteousness" as going to be filled.[2]

All the synoptic narratives of the Last Supper include references to Jesus' expectation of drinking wine in the kingdom of God (Mark 14:25, Matthew 26:29, Luke 22:18). Luke adds a reference to the future paschal meal (22:15-16) and represents Jesus as "deeding" a kingdom to his apostles so that they may "eat and drink at my table in my kingdom" (22:29-30; Matthew 19:28, with a similar context, lacks such references). Conceivably Paul reinterprets something like the whole Lucan picture in 1 Corinthians 4:8. "Have you already been filled? Are you already rich? Are you kings apart from us?" Perhaps the Corinthians have taken something like the Lucan passages in relation to the "knowledge" that exalts them. Paul treats them literally simply to show that on this basis they are incredible. In actual fact they are both symbolic and eschatological, as he indicates in other contexts. "Flesh and blood cannot inherit the kingdom of God" (1 Cor. 15:50); "the kingdom of God is not food and drink but righteousness and peace and joy in the Holy Spirit" (Romans 14:17).

Apocalyptic eschatology did not fade away in the second century. Justin, about 150, claimed that "I and whoever others are Christians orthodox (ὀρθογνώμονες) in every respect, know that there will be a resurrection of the flesh and a period of a thousand years in a Jerusalem built up and beautified and enlarged, as the prophets Ezekiel and Isaiah, like the others, acknowledge" (*Dial.* 80.5). They were not Justin's only authorities. "John, one of the apostles of Christ, predicted in the revelation which he had that those who believed in our Christ would have a thousand years in Jerusalem" (*Dial.* 81.4). Irenaeus insisted that the promises were not to be taken allegorically and the events would take place on earth (v. 35.1-2). He makes this statement in the course of a long section on promises (v. 32-36) in the course of which he accepts extravagant promises related by Papias of Hierapolis. We shall shortly come to these matters.

Suffice it now to refer to Tertullian's claim that the heavenly Jerusalem nearly came down to earth in about the year 200. Over Judaea it appeared for forty days before dawn, but would then vanish at sunrise. Origen, on the other hand, insists that when the Son of Man appears it will not be in any particular location. Dionysius of Alexandria raised questions about the apostolicity of the Apocalypse of John, using older sources to criticize the

---

[2] Clement of Alexandria (*Quis dives* 17.4) says that Matthew added the words "for righteousness" in order to clarify the meaning of "hunger and thirst," just as he added "in spirit" to "poor." Origen sharply criticizes those who fail to understand that all such passages must be interpreted spiritually (*De princ.* ii. 11.2).

"wedding of the Lamb" as consisting of a thousand years of feasting and reigning (Rev. 19:9, 20:4).[3]

The tension between apocalyptic and non-apocalyptic spirituality continued in the later third century and the fourth, not to mention still later periods. Here we mention the apocalyptists, Commodian, Methodius, and Victorinus, whose *Commentary on the Apocalypse* was later de-eschatologized by Jerome (CSEL 49). There is also the case of Eusebius, who seems to have de-eschatologized himself.[4] Our best witness for continuing apocalyptic thought is probably the tutor of Constantine's son, Lactantius, who self-consciously argued that biblical predictions were confirmed by Hermes Trismegistus and the Sibyl but especially by "the most ancient King of the Medes, Hystaspes."[5] The passage that concerns us is this (vii. 24.7; Bidez-Cumont 374-75):[6]

> The earth will open up its fertility and generate the richest fruits spontaneously, mountain cliffs will flow with honey, wine will flow down in streams, and rivers will overflow with milk.... Then will take place what poets said occurred in the golden times, long ago in the reign of Saturn.

BREAD TOMORROW

Jewish and Christian apocalyptic authors found great quantities of bread and wine promised in the imminent age to come. Their starting point, or one of their starting points, seems to lie, as Rendel Harris long ago suggested, in the wording of Isaac's blessing in Genesis 27:28.[7] "May God give you...plenty (רֹב) of grain and wine." Any ingenious rabbinic commentator, like Harris, would have found it easy to substitute רִבֵּי (ten thousand) for the original "plenty." He would simply be explaining what the text meant.

---

[3]Tertullian, *Adv. Marc.* iii. 24.4; Origen, *Matt. ser.* 70; Eusebius, *H. E.* vii. 25.3; cf. iii. 28.2, 5.

[4]*Eusebius as Church Historian* (Oxford 1980).

[5]*Inst.* vii. 15.19; Bidez-Cumont, *Les Mages hellénisés*, II 366; cf. R. M. Ogilvie, *The Library of Lactantius* (Oxford 1978).

[6]Note also that in the *Orat. ad sanct. coetum* (21.1) ascribed to Constantine the fourth *Eclogue* of Vergil is expounded as concerning Christ and the passages dealing with miraculous fertility are viewed as pointing to the power of God. On problems in Lactantius' thought cf. L. J. Swift, "Lactantius and the Golden Age," *American Journal of Philology* 89 (1968), 144-56.

[7]"A New Patristic Fragment," *Expositor* ser. V. vol. 1 (1895), 448-55, esp. 449.

Thus in 1 Enoch 10:29 we find thousandfold returns from seeds sown on the regenerated earth, while 2 Baruch 29:5 tells us that "the earth will give its fruits ten thousand for one." The early Jewish Christian Papias of Hierapolis says that a grain of wheat will produce ten thousand ears, one ear will have ten thousand grains, and one grain will produce five 2-pound units of flour. His testimony is reproduced by Irenaeus (*Adv. haer.* v. 33.3). If Rousseau--Doutreleau--Mercier are right in turning *bilibres* into χούνικας (*Sources chrétiennes* 153, 417), and if the χοῖνιξ was really equivalent to about a liter, we then have a crop returning five hundred million to one or, indeed, considerably more--if the text has been correctly transmitted.

We should also refer to the rabbinic notion that in the future "wheat will rise as high as a palm-tree and will grow on the top of the mountains" (Bab. Kethuboth 111b, p. 721 Slotki). This notion apparently underlies the picture in the Christian Didache of bread as once "scattered upon the mountains," then gathered and becoming one (ix. 4). The picture is of a miraculous crop, not an ordinary one. So is the "bread of tomorrow," prayed for in the Lord's Prayer in the Gospel according to the Hebrews.

WINE TOMORROW

In the eschatological prediction of 1 Enoch 10:19 we find that in the last time the vines to be planted would produce ten thousand πρόχοι of wine. The editor of CIG 5641-5642 (cf. IG XIV 421-422) suggested that a πρόχους was the same as a χοῦς. If a κάδος of twelve πρόχοι contained about twenty liters (CIG III p. 649; H. Chantraine in *KP* III 42-43), the product was about 16667 liters. On the other hand, if the πρόχους was 1/12 of a κοτύλη (L. Gry in *Vivre et Penser* 3, 1943/4, 117) figured at 0.24 liter, we get only 200 liters of wine (cf. Chantraine in *KP* III 320). We are happy to pass on to the apocalypse known as 2 Baruch, in which we find that "each vine will bear a thousand shoots, each shoot will bear a thousand clusters, each cluster will bear a thousand grapes, and each grape will produce a *kor* of wine" (29:5). Since each vine would bear a billion grapes, our uncertainty about the *kor* (perhaps about 365 liters) is irrelevant. Beyond 2 Baruch lies the early Jewish Christian Papias of Hierapolis, who according to Irenaeus (v. 33.3) expected each vine to produce 10,000 shoots, each shoot 10,000 branches, each branch 10,000 twigs, each twig 10,000 clusters, and each cluster 10,000 grapes. Finally each grape would produce twenty-five μετρηταί of wine. Begin with the vine and proceed to the grapes: the product reaches the astounding total of one hundred quintillion. If now we consider the twenty-five μετρηταί, each at about forty liters, we reach a still more astounding hundred sextillion liters. Small wonder that in a similar account related by Hippolytus (*Dan.* iv. 60.1) we hear only that the Lord told his disciples that the future kingdom of the saints would be "glorious and marvelous." Clement of Alexandria was no apocalyptist anyway, but as a moralist he condemned any more than "a little wine" (*Paed.* ii. 19-34; 1 Tim. 5:23). Eusebius thought that Papias was stupid and given to fantasy; he had misled Irenaeus (*H. E.* iii. 39.11-13). In writing on *The Greek Patristic View of Nature* (Manchester 1968), D. S. Wallace-Hadrill does not mention any such notions.

FIGS TOMORROW

Beyond bread and wine lie figs. Unlike other plants, the fig tree is mentioned in the gospel chiefly because of its failure to produce. It therefore might be regarded as a prime example of plants, as symbols, condemned in the judgment to come.[8] One could imagine other circumstances; thus there were no figs in Jerusalem in the famine of 46/47, when they had to be imported from Cyprus (Josephus, *Ant*. xx. 51).

The basic problem arises out of Mark's presentation of the story. "As they were coming from Bethany he was hungry. And seeing from a distance a fig tree in leaf he came to find what might be on it. And when he came to it he found nothing but leaves, for it was not the season for figs. He responded by saying to it, 'May no one ever eat fruit from you.' And his disciples heard it" (11:12-14). That evening, on the way back to Bethany, the disciples note that the fig tree has withered, and Peter draws Jesus' attention to the fact. Jesus replies to him with a series of calls to faith in the future as the time when God will give gifts (11:20-25).

Whether or not the eschatological sayings have anything to do with the situation,[9] the setting of the story is plain. A hungry Jesus wants figs, a staple of Palestinian diet, even though they are out of season. Leaves have appeared but no fruit. The reaction of cursing the fig tree seems excessive. So, at least, it would have appeared to Epictetus, who speaks of the foolishness of longing for figs in wintertime (*Diss*. iii. 24.86-87) and is echoed by Marcus Aurelius (xi. 33): "Only a madman expects a fig in winter." Even the Christian Hippolytus urges readers of the scriptures not to be "hasty or rash" like one who would desire to see the green fruits of the figtree "before the time" (*Dan*. iv. 15.1). Considerations of this sort have led to the revision of the story in pre-Marcan tradition and in Luke.[10]

Pre-Marcan tradition (unless we are dealing with Mark's own composition) accounts for the "parable" or comparison of Mark 13:28. "From the fig tree learn the comparison: as soon as its branch becomes tender and puts forth its leaves, you know that summer is near." If this is a version of the cursing story, obviously all the sting has been taken out. The editorial activity of the evangelist Luke has done even more. As J. M. Creed pointed out in his commentary (London [1930] 239), "Luke has omitted the incident of the cursing of the unfruitful fig-tree, and the sayings of which it was the occasion in Mark. He almost certainly read it in Mark (cf. xvii. 6...), and for obvious reasons preferred to discard it." First of all, Luke replaced the story with a parable (13:6-9).

---

[8] Examples cited by A. de Q. Robin in *NTS* 8, 1961/2, 279-80.

[9] See my article in *JBL* 67 (1948) 297-303.

[10] On fig cultivation see e.g., Pliny xviii. 245 and Columella v. 10.10.

> A man had a fig tree planted in his vineyard; and he came
> seeking fruit on it and found none. And he said to the
> vinedresser, "Lo, these three years I have come seeking
> fruit on this fig tree, and I find none. Cut it down;
> why should it use up the ground?" And he answered him,
> "Let it alone, sir, this year also, till I dig about it
> and put on manure. And if it bears fruit next year, well
> and good; but if not, you can cut it down."

Here is a moralizing picture of Israel and a tree not necessarily to be condemned. Naturally the anti-Jewish Marcion deleted it from his Gospel (Harnack, *Marcion* 217*) while Irenaeus treated the expected fruit as justice (iv. 36.8). Second, Luke takes one of the companion sayings on faith (Mark 11:22-23) and rewrites it thus (Luke 17:6): "If you had faith in a grain of mustard seed, you could say to this sycamine [fig] tree, 'Be rooted up and planted in the sea' and it would obey you" (compare Matthew 17:20).

The embarrassing features of the early story, as well as its possible reference to eschatological events, have been removed.[11] We are on our way to Origen, who treats the fig tree as the Jewish people without any qualification. The story has no "literal" meaning, since the fig tree is "the tree of the people" and Jesus addresses it as animate (*Matthew comm.* xvi. 26, pp. 561-64 Klostermann, esp. 561, 18--562, 15). Methodius takes a different route. He gives a highly allegorical analysis of figs, which for sweetness and beauty resemble the food of paradise, but does not refer to the cursing (*Symp.* x. 5). The unpleasant features of the gospel story have been left behind. Fig trees can grow in tombs, he says when writing *On the resurrection* (ii. 9.9); this fact symbolizes God's resurrective power.

PAST AND PRESENT CEREALS AND FRUITS

Sometimes it is supposed that expectations of miraculous feedings are due to looking backward to a distant past, whether in regard to Eden or in regard to the land of promise offered to Moses. Certainly the spies of Moses "cut down from the Valley of Eshcol 'cluster' a branch with a single cluster of grapes, and they carried it on a pole between two of them; they also brought some pomegranates and figs" (Num. 13:23). They described the land as "flowing with milk and honey" (13:27). According to Deuteronomy 8:79, Moses said it was well irrigated, "a land of wheat and barley, of vines and fig-trees and pomegranates, a land of olive trees and honey, a land in which you will eat bread without scarcity, in which you will lack nothing."

In the first century, however, there was no reason for looking back nostalgically to the days of the conquest of Canaan. Josephus describes part of the promised land, i.e., the plain of Gennesaret, northwest of the Lake of

---

[11]Similarly any possible eschatological reference to "this mountain" (Zech. 14.4) in Mark 11:23 disappears in Paul's idea of faith that moves mountains (1 Cor. 13:2). Matthew 21:19 simplifies. In Luke's view the disciples did not understand eschatology (18:34, 19:11).

Galilee, as wonderfully productive in his own time (*Bell.* iii. 516-21). "There is not a plant which its fertile soil refuses to produce, and its cultivators in fact grow every species." He mentions walnuts, palms, figs, and olives. "For ten months without intermission the country supplies the best of fruits, the grape and the fig: the rest mature on the trees the whole year round."

Now we take a look at some "parables of growth" in the gospels. Do they express a yearning for a rate of growth well beyond what was thought possible?

The evangelist Mark provides us with three parables of growth, one about seeds sown in four kinds of soil (4:3-8), another aobut a sown seed growing spontaneously (4:26-29), and a third about the impressive growth of the mustard seed (4:30-32). We assume, though nothing is said of it, that Jesus would have agreed with the apostle Paul: human agents plant and sometimes bring water, but "God gives the growth" (1 Cor. 3:6). Thus it is God who out of "the smallest of all seeds" produces a plant "greater than all other vegetables." Pliny makes a similar point. "It grows entirely wild...but when it has once been sown it is scarcely possible to get the place free of it, as the seed when it falls germinates at once" (*N. H.* xix. 170; in five days according to Theophrastus vii. 1.3). Since mustard was a medicine and a relish we shall not discuss it further. As for another seed with remarkable growth, after the sower casts it on the earth it buds and sprouts, he knows not how. "The earth produces fruit spontaneously (αὐτομάτη)-- first the stalk, then the ear, then the full grain in the ear." The language reminds us of Golden Age language, but is being applied to the ordinary agricultural situation. This situation is not dependent on human observation or activity. God gives the growth.

For our purposes the most important of these parables has to do with the productivity of various soils, notably the results when seed falls on good earth. Then the seeds "come up and grow and produce thirtyfold, sixtyfold, and a hundredfold." We may note that Luke simplifies, mentioning only the largest return (8:8), while in the Gospel of Thomas (Log. 9), love of symmetry results in multiplication by sixty and one hundred and twenty. The "hundred" figure had a worthy precedent. When Isaac was living in the land of the Philistines, he "sowed in that land, and reaped in the same year a hundredfold" (Gen. 26:12). Similarly in the Infancy story of Thomas, Jesus was out sowing with his father and himself sowed one grain of wheat. When he had reaped it and threshed it, he brought in a hundred *kors*;[12] and he called all the poor of the village to the threshing-floor and gave them the wheat, and Joseph took the residue of the wheat. "He was eight years old when he worked the miracle" p. 396 Hennecke-Schneemelcher; p. 151 Tischendorf). It is possible that a similar miracle story was once legible in Bell and Skeat's *Fragments of an Unknown Gospel* (frag. 2 verso) where Jesus was certainly depicted as sowing, but the papyrus has too many gaps for us to be sure.

---

[12]If we take the *kor* at 300 liters (SC 145, 63) we reach 30,000 liters.

We need say little about the spiritual interpretation of these yields. It develops out of the "many abodes" mentioned in John 14:2 when these are taken with three levels of reward. The hundreds live in heaven, sixties in paradise, thirties in the new Jerusalem (Irenaeus v. 36.2; cf. Clement., *Str.* vi. 114.3). Or one might identify hundreds as martyrs, sixties as virgins, thirties as widows (Origen, *Jos. hom.* ii. 1; cf. *Gen. hom.* xii. 5). None of this has anything to do with the agricultural setting of the parable.

What sort of return is being envisaged? The highest yield I have seen reported or claimed is three hundred on barley, mentioned by Strabo (742) for Babylon. Pliny (xviii. 162) agrees with Theophrastus (viii. 7.4) in assigning yields of fifty or a hundred on wheat in the area. At the western end of the Mediterranean Baetica in southern Spain was thought to return a hundred on wheat (Pliny xviii. 95), while the same figure is given for southeastern Italy (Varro i. 44.2), eastern Tunisia (Varro; 150 in Pliny xviii. 94-95), Egypt (Pliny xviii. 95; only 70 in Ammianus Marcellinus xxii. 15.13), and Syria near Gadara (Varro). These figures obviously represent exaggerated or freakish situations. More normally the return might be fourfold (Columella iii. 3.4), fivefold (Bab. Kethuboth 112a, p. 726 Slotki), or even from eight to fifteen (Varro; Cicero, *In Verr.* ii. 3.112). Exceptional returns of thirty are mentioned for Sicilian vegetables by Theophrastus (viii. 2.8) and for Crimean wheat by Strabo (311). It is therefore evident that returns of thirty, sixty, and a hundred were what Greeks and Romans who discussed agricultural yields considered exceptional.[13]

How abnormal they were is clear from Edward Crankshaw's *Shadow of the Winter Palace* (New York 1976), p. 293, in reliance on Richard Pipes, *Russia under the Old Regime* (London 1974):

> In medieval Europe the typical yield was expressed in the ratio 1:3-- three grains harvested for each grain sown. By the sixteenth and seventeenth centuries this ratio had improved to 1:6 or 1:7. By the middle of the nineteenth century the yield in England was 1:10. But the Russian yield still averaged 1:3.

MULTIPLICATION OF BREAD (AND FISH)

The multiplication of wheat for bread was not confined to the distant past, the remote provinces, or the uncertain future. According to all four gospels, the time of Jesus was the time of the renewal of prophecy and miracle. The particular prophetic miracle now renewed is described in 2 Kings 4:42-44. An admirer brought Elisha "bread of the first fruits, twenty loaves of barley, and fresh ears of grain in his sack." Could this offering suffice to feed a hundred men? Elisha ordered it given to them, "that they may eat, for thus says the Lord, 'They shall eat and have some left.'" The same ideas recur in the Feeding of the Five Thousand (Mark 6:31-44 and parallels) and its pendant

---

[13] Cf. G. Rickman, *The Corn Supply of Ancient Rome* (Oxford 1980) 103.

(Mark 8:1-9). It is late as Jesus teaches a crowd. Two hundred denarii worth of bread[14] is not available. Fortunately there are five loaves and two fish. When blessed and distributed, this is enough for all who eat. "And they took up twelve baskets full of broken pieces and of the fish." To put this statistically, it would appear that the bread was multiplied by about a thousand.

The evangelist John prefers to meditate upon the meaning of another miraculous feeding in the Old Testament, this one the gift of manna in the wilderness of Sin. "A fine, flake-like thing, fine as hoarfrost on the ground" turned out to be "the bread which the Lord has given you to eat." Twice as much was gathered on the sixth day so that on the Sabbath, when the manna did not arrive, food would be available (Exodus 16:14-36). According to John, Jesus proceeds to identify this as bread from heaven (cf. "bread of the angels," Ps. 78:25) but inferior to himself, the true "bread of God who descends from heaven and gives life to the world" (John 6:32-35) or even the flesh and blood of Jesus (6:51c-58). Various aspects of the manna could of course be emphasized. Philo points out that God chose to produce food out of the air instead of rain (*Mos.* i. 202).

One seems to see a spiritualizing of this kind of miracle in several Christian circles. Thus Paul insists upon at least the spiritual meaning of the manna. "They all ate the same spiritual food, and all drank the same spiritual drink; for they drank from the spiritual rock that followed them, and the rock was Christ" (1 Cor. 10: 3-4; Philonic parallels in J. Weiss, *Komm.* 250-51). Again, the Didachist thanks God for the gift of food and drink to mankind in general, for spiritual food and drink to Christians (10:3). And finally Ignatius speaks of deacons "of the mysteries of Jesus Christ" who must "please all in every way" (cf. 1 Cor. 10:33). They are not ministers of food and drink but servants of the church of God (*Trall.* 2:3). Presumably their ministry is eucharistic and the eucharist is spiritual; it has little to do with ordinary meals. A line earlier blurred is getting clearer. Clement interprets the five barley loaves as preliminary instruction and the fish as philosophy; or else the two fish are the encyclia and philosophy (*Str.* vi. 94.2-5).

A variant of the Feeding of the Five Thousand appears in the apocryphal *Acts of John* (93 Bonnet, E. T. p. 227 Hennecke et al.). Whenever Jesus received a dinner invitation from one of the Pharisees (characteristically Lucan: 7:36, 11:37, 14:1) and he accepted it (for the option, 1 Cor. 10:27), all his disciples went with him. "One loaf was set before each by the hosts, and Jesus also would take one; but he would bless his and divide it among us; and every man was satisfied by that little piece, and our own loaves were kept intact, so that those who had invited him were amazed."

The idea that Jesus' disciples accompanied him to dinners may be implied by the traditions in their Lucan setting. Perhaps it is more significant that according to John 2:2 both Jesus and his disciples were invited to the wedding

---

[14] 3200 ordinary loaves or twice as many small loaves; cf. F. W. Heichelheim in T. Frank, *Economic Survey of Ancient Rome*, IV 184).

at Cana in Galilee--"where he made the water wine" (4:46).

Oddly enough, the author of the *Acts of John* goes on to say that "his miracles and wonderful works must not be told for the moment, for they are unspeakable and perhaps cannot be uttered or heard." This seems odd because several have just been described.

Not much attention seems to be given the fish of the feeding-miracles, but they have a special role to play in other accounts. Since according to the rabbis "a meal without fish is no meal" (Ber. 44a, p. 268 M. Simon[15]), and since in the *Testament of Zebulon* vi. 6 God is described as instrumental in a good catch with a net, we should expect to hear about catching fish.[16] Actual practice on the lake of Galilee seems to be depicted in the parable of the Drag Net (Matt. 13:47-50), where all the fish are kept until the net is landed. A similar point occurs in the Gospel of Thomas (log. 8), where the fisherman keeps a large good fish and throws little ones back. (The eschatological point has been blunted.) At the feedings of the Five and Four Thousand, fish are multiplied without emphasis. And after the resurrection Jesus eats a piece of fish according to Luke (24:42-43) or cooks some for his disciples according to John (21:9, 13).

Miraculous, or at least remarkable, catches of fish are described by Luke and John. According to Luke (5:1-11) Simon has fished all night without result, but Jesus told him where to let down his nets. The consequence was a catch that filled two boats so that they almost sank. Similarly in John at the end of a night Jesus gives directions and the net can barely be brought in. There are 153 large fish in it (21:1-14). Conceivably the point is numerological, since 153 is the sum of all the numbers to seventeen, itself the sum of the significant numbers ten and seven. In any case it has nothing to do with possible species of fish.[17]

It cannot be said that fish are as significant as bread and wine in the life of the church militant or at rest. According to 2 Baruch 29:4 Behemoth and Leviathan (the latter from the deep, cf. Ps. 104:26) will serve as food in the messianic age. Leviathan, however, is a gigantic monster rather than a fish. It may be that Behemoth is a hippopotamus or a crocodile, Leviathan a crocodile or a whale (Hastings DB[2], 95a). In any case, no one seems to have used either for food.

Only in the Gospel of John do we hear of Jesus as the Vine (with disciples as branches) or encounter the sudden production of large quantities of wine at Cana. The evangelist makes much of this "beginning of signs"

---

[15] Some manuscripts read "salt" for "fish"; cf. S-B I 684 n. a and 1.

[16] Subject discussed more economically and theologically by W. H. Wuellner, *The Meaning of Fishers of Men* (Philadelphia 1967) 11-63.

[17] *HTR* 42, 1949, 273-75.

performed there, when Jesus "manifested his glory and his disciples believed in him" (2:11; cf. 4:46). The scene is depicted in the first seven verses, in which we find out that at a wedding all the wine has been consumed, and the servants are told to fill "six stone water jars...each holding two or three μετρηταί." This means that each held 80 or 120 liters and the total amount was 480 or 720 liters. The water secretly transforms itself into wine of high quality, on which the bridegroom receives compliments. "People generally set out the good wine first...you have kept the good wine till now" (2:10). Just so, Pliny criticizes hosts who give guests "other wines than those served to themselves, or else substitute inferior wines as the meal progresses" (xiv. 91).

The three earliest Christian commentators on this miracle story take it to be historical.[18] Irenaeus adds that though the Lord could have made wine out of nothing he preferred to show his relation to the God who created water (Gen. 1:9). The miracle is new or renovated creation like the old.

To be sure, Pliny tells of a vine at Rome in the porticoes of Livia that covered the walks with its trellises and produced twelve *amphorae* of juice per year, or roughly 300 liters (xiv. 11). Columella had a neighbor, perhaps in Etruria, for whom a vine "miraculously" produced 2000 clusters (iii. 3.3). These examples are less impressive than the Johannine story, which has better parallels in the cult of Dionysus.

At Teos near Smyrna, on the island of Andros, and at Elis in the western Peloponnese, the changing of water into wine on fixed occasions revealed the power and presence of the god Dionysus. It was said that Dionysus was born at Teos because at set times a fountain of wine spontaneously flowed from the ground in the city (Diodorus Siculus iii. 66.2). In the vicinity of Elis, according to the fourth-century historian Theopompus, natives were accustomed to seal three bronze cauldrons, all empty, in the presence of visitors to the Dionysia. They were opened later and found full of wine (Athenaeus 34a; cf. [Arist.] *De mirab. auscult,* 123; Pausanias vi. 26.1). And in the temple of Dionysus on Andros wine flowed from a fountain every year for the week beginning January 5, a day called "God's gift." If the wine was removed from the temple it turned back into water (Pliny ii. 231; xxxi. 16; Pausanias vi. 26.2 [doubts]; Philostratus, *Imag.* i. 25). Campbell Bonner long ago suspected that a similar miracle was regularly provided by means of a tunnel leading to a temple in Corinth,[19] and it seems likely that Christians at Gerasa (Jerash) in Jordan based their repetition of the miracle on an older Dionysiac tradition in the same location.[20] Epiphanius says that in the fourth century the transformation was still taking place in "many" areas (li. 30.1-2).

Others seem to have tried to solve the discrepancy between literal and

---

[18]Irenaeus iii. 11.5; Clement, *Paed.* ii. 29.1; Origen, *Ioh. comm.* xiii. 64.

[19]"A Dionysiac Miracle in Corinth," *AJA* 33 (1929) 368-75.

[20]C. H. Kraeling, ed., *Gerasa: City of the Decapolis* (New Haven 1938), 37, 63-64, 201, 210-12.

spiritual by means of magic. Irenaeus knew a Gnostic teacher named Marcus who was accustomed to perform two magical tricks in the course of his so-called eucharist (i. 13.2). First, he would take a cup of wine mixed with water and by means of a protracted invocation would make it appear "purple and red"-- presumably this means "purple or red," though Epiphanius tells of three separate cups, all with white wine that turned red, purple, and blue (SC 263, 241)! The original colors were supposed to come from the blood of the "Grace from the regions above all." Hippolytus (Ref. vi. 38.3) explains that he slipped a drug (a mixture of indigo and frankincense, iv. 28.13) into the mixture. The long invocation gave the drug time to dissolve.

More interestingly, he would have a woman give thanks over a cup of mixed wine and then pour the contents into a much larger cup. He would pray thus: "May that Grace which is before everything unthinkable and ineffable, fill your inner man and multiply her knowledge in you, sowing the mustard seed on good earth." Since the mustard seed comes from a parable of growth and is combined with the good earth that produces huge crops, it is no wonder that the small cup would fill the larger one -- even to overflowing, as in the case of the divine gift mentioned in Luke 6:38. Hippolytus once more betrays skepticism. He says there are "many drugs" (presumably effervescent powders) that can produce such effects, though he does not name them. He adds that the Marcosians poured the wine back and forth from one cup to the other and, as air got in the water, wine bubbled up. Since it would not remain bubbly for long, the bystanders had to drink it at once (vi. 40.3-4).

Another Gnostic woman, Philumene, friend of the Marcionite Apelles, was accustomed to put a large loaf of bread into a glass bottle with a very narrow mouth and then lift it out undamaged with her fingertips. This was the only food she ate, in a semi-divine fashion.[21]

POSSIBLE PAGAN FRAMEWORKS

How would literate pagan readers or hearers take stories and notions like these? The most obvious parallels occur in poetic accounts of the Golden Age or the Isles of the Blest. We begin with the Golden Race described by Hesiod in his *Works and Days* (109-20), probably about 700 B.C. Though mortal, these people were exempt from sadness and work. They feasted steadily, "for the fruitful earth spontaneously and ungrudgingly bore fruit for them." Hesiod himself was aware of living in a fifth period with an Iron Race, involved in labor and grief by day, destruction by night (176-78). Even so, work in the fields prevents famine and disaster, for "the earth brings forth much sustenance" (230-32). But you must work with work upon work (382); as Vergil put it, "Labor omnia vicit" (*Georg*. i. 145). Vergil earlier describes the age of Saturn when "no tillers subdued the land" and there was no private property. "Men made gain for the common store, and earth herself brought forth all things more freely when none demanded them." In addition, "wine ran everywhere in streams" (*Georg*. i. 125-32). In his famous *Eclogue IV* he predicts that the reign of Saturn is returning; the

---

[21]A. v. Harnack, *Marcion: das Evangelium vom fremden Gott* (TU 45, Leipzig 1924) 408-9*.

untilled earth will pour forth gifts and "every land will bear all fruits" (39). No dyes will be needed because rams will change the color of their fleeces to purple or yellow, while lambs will turn scarlet (43-45). Horace ventures to say that no better ruler than Augustus has existed or will exist, even if the Golden Age should return (*Od.* iv. 2.37-40). Earlier he had thought of escaping, around the time of Actium, to the Isles of the Blest, where "the unploughed land yields grain and the unpruned vine always blooms." It is a place where one can recover the charm of the Golden Age (*Epod.* 16). Still later Ovid too tells how "the untilled earth brought forth her fruits," especially wheat, and streams flowed with milk and nectar (*Met.* i. 109-11).

We have mentioned the Isles of the Blest, and we should note Lucian's description in his *True Stories*--in which he parodies historians and states that "I am writing about things which I have neither seen nor had to do with nor learned from others, things which, in fact, do not exist at all and, in the nature of things, cannot exist" (i. 4). Anyway, on the Isles of the Blest "the grape vines yield twelve vintages a year, bearing every month; the pomegranates, apples and other fruit trees were said to bear thirteen times a year, for in one month, their Minoan, they bear twice. Instead of wheat-ears, loaves of bread all baked grow on the tops of the wheat, so that they look like mushrooms. About the city there are 365 springs of water, as many of honey, 500 of myrrh (much smaller, however), and seven rivers of milk and eight of wine" (ii. 13).

More sedately, Lucian tells us how the poets described the Golden Age: the earth produced its good things for the folk without sowing and without ploughing, an ample meal ready to each man's hand; the rivers flowed, some with wine, some with milk, and other again with honey" (*Sat.* 20). But then, even in the early empire the poem *Aetna* (9-16) had explained that in the Golden Age "no one sowed wheat in plowed fields or kept weeds out of the future crops, but brimming harvests yearly filled the granaries." More miraculously, "the wine pressed itself...."

Obtaining large quantities of wine without effort or cost was also a mark of the Golden Age (e.g., *Aetna* 13; Lucian, *Saturnalia* 7) or of the Happy Isles (Horace, *Epod.* xvi. 44) or of the Elysian Fields (Lucian, *Ver. Hist.* ii. 14). In the last version, naturally a parody, glass trees bear glass cups which, when picked, "immediately fill with wine."

Vergil, Horace, and Ovid give us relatively serious pictures of how one might imagine the Golden Age (etc.) to have been, Lucian by no means so serious. Indeed, Lucian might be the link back (via Athenaeus) to the absurdities of the "burlesques of the Golden Age" culled by Athenaeus from the remains of poets of the fifth-century Old Comedy (267E-270A),[22] which carry us farther into the world of fantasy and miracle. Crates introduced self-moving furniture and allowed people to speak thus: "Walk this way, my

---

[22] Cf. E. L. Green, "The Land of Cockaigne in Attic Comedy," *TAPA* 34 (1903), xxxii; C. Bonner, "Dionysiac Magic and the Greek Land of Cockaigne," *TAPA* 41 (1910) 175-85.

barley-cake," and to converse with fish. Here the scene seems to be future.

"Fish, get up!"

"But I'm not yet done on the other side!"

"Well, turn yourself over, won't you? and baste yourself with oil and salt."

But in the *Amphictyons* of Telecleides it is Cronus who speaks of the Golden Age which he provided for mortals, when "things needful existed spontaneously." For example, "every torrent flowed with wine, barley-cakes strove with wheat-cakes for men's lips, beseeching that they be swallowed if men loved the whitest." In addition, "fish would come to the house and bake themselves, then serve themselves on the tables." Perhaps further quotations are unnecessary.

Given the parallels between the basic pictures and the Genesis account of Eden, it is small wonder that they were used to fill out the scriptural narrative. Often it is hard to tell which kind of story is being told. Take Philo in the *De opificio mundi* (79-81). When man was created he found in Eden "all provisions for life." "Nature seemed almost to cry aloud in so many words that like the first father of the race men were to spend their days without toil or trouble, surrounded by lavish abundance of all that they needed." But now because of sin men have to work incessantly. If the situation changes (as Philo expects it will, *Praem.* 101-3, 168) God will provide for our race "good things all coming forth spontaneously and all in readiness."

Beyond the absurdities of the land of Cockaigne, where amiable nature serves man's good pleasure and his sense of the cosmic, lies the idiotic Gnostic picture of a nature weary of age-old violations, protesting to the baptist sectarian Elchasai and his disciples, as cited by Mani.[23]

> Mani said again that Elchasai found his disciples baking bread. The bread spoke with Elchassai, and he commanded them to bake no longer. Again Mani points out that Sabbaios, the Baptist, was carrying vegetables to the elder of the city. And immediately that produce said to him: "Are you not righteous? Are you not pure? Why do you carry us away to the fornicators?" Thus Sabbaios was upset on account of what he heard and returned the vegetables. Again Mani points out that a date-palm tree spoke with Aianos, the Baptist from Koche, and commanded him to say to its lord, "Don't cut me down because my fruit is stolen, but grant me this year. And in the course of this year I shall give you fruit proportionate to

---

[23] R. Cameron--A. J. Dewey (trs.). *The Cologne Mani Codex* (SBL Texts and Translations 15, 1979), 79 (papyrus, pp. 97-99).

what has been stolen, and in all the other years
hereafter." But it also commanded him to say to
that man who was stealing its fruit: "Do not come
at this season to steal my fruit away. If you come,
I shall hurl you down from my height and you will die."

No doubt further messages await on the last 93 pages of the Mani Codex. Meanwhile we simply note that the last conversation resembles the one between a man and his vinedresser (Luke 13:6-9) to which we have already referred. What was human even if perhaps eschatological in Luke has become fantastic, even sentimental, in the Elchasaite version. And instead of the comedy of Cockaigne we encounter the grim mania not of Mani but of the sectarians whom even he had the good sense to reject.

CONCLUSION

This paper is not intended to provide directly any final or theological solution of the problems raised by the tension between literal-miraculous and more spiritual interpretations of the miraculous feedings past, present and future. Some intimations may have been provided along the way, and we add a few more in conclusion, and as alternatives. (1) There is the idea of a continuing providential productivity, to be found in 1 Clement 20, whether Stoic or mediately Jewish or not. "The earth brings forth at proper seasons according to God's will and raises abundant food for men and beasts and everything that lives on it.... The ever-flowing springs, created for enjoyment and health, unfailingly offer their breasts for the life of mankind." Werner Jaeger thought he saw a fragment from Greek tragedy underlying these passages.[24] That would not make them any less Christian. (2) There is the notion of work in cooperation with God to which we have already referred (1 Cor. 3:6). It is conceivable that Paul did not say, "If anyone will not work, let him not eat" (2 Thess. 3:10). But there is quite enough in his letters to undergird a gospel of work (e.g., 1 Thess. 4:11-12). (3) Finally, with real famines not uncommon,[25] the notion of "sending relief, every one according to his ability" (Acts 11:29) seems significant. Though Origen, like Dionysius of Alexandria and the Hermetic *Asclepius*, can envisage food shortages in the imminent future, he does not expect them to be ended by miracle.[26] Christians like others have come to regard the promises of miraculous feeding as possessed of spiritual, not material, meanings.

---

[24] Rh Mus 102 (1959) 330-40.

[25] Cf. R. MacMullen, *Enemies of the Roman Order* (Cambridge, Mass. 1966) 249-54.

[26] Origen, *Matt. ser.* 36; Dionysius in Eusebius, *H. E.* vii. 21. Christians did not expect to duplicate the miracles of feeding.

Response by Peter R. L. Brown, Professor of History and Classics
University of California, Berkeley

In this elegant and sensible study, Robert Grant has introduced us, with his habitual clarity and restraint, to an important strand in the imagination of Mediterranean and Near Eastern men: the dream of abundance. The study makes us realize, also, how very rapidly this dream came to be dismissed as a disreputable fantasy by articulate leaders of Christian opinion. Eusebius cited with evident approval the answer of Dionysios of Alexandria to the Egyptian bishop, Nepos, "who taught that the promises made to the saints in holy scripture would be fulfilled more in accordance with Jewish ideas, and suggested that there would be a millennium of bodily indulgence on this earth."[1] "The things he lusted after himself [wrote Dionysios of the bishop's source, Cerinthus], being the slave of his body and sensual through and through, filled the heaven of his dreams--unlimited indulgence in gluttony and lechery at banquets, drinking bouts and wedding-feasts."[2] Yet even for Eusebius, old images of delight floated close to the surface. The awe-inspiring pomp of the Imperial banquet that followed the Council of Nicaea provoked an entirely appropriate reverie:

> Detachments of the body-guard and troops surrounded the entrance of the palace with drawn swords, and through the midst of these the men of God proceeded without fear into the innermost of the Imperial apartments, in which some were the Emperor's companions at table, while others reclined on couches arranged on either side. One might have thought that a picture of Christ's kingdom was thus shadowed forth, and a dream rather than reality.[3]

"Food and drink" (Rom. 14:17)--in the words of an acute reader of Rabelais, "The mighty aspiration to abundance and to a universal spirit"[4] were not so easily banished from the kingdom of God. The process by which such imagery came to be eliminated was a long and complicated one, and the consequent sterilization of the imagination of the Christian church was not necessarily a gain for good sense. It certainly did not contribute to good relations with the neighbors of Western Europe. The almost total incomprehension displayed by later Christians when faced, in the Islamic description of Paradise, with an eschatology as majestic and as serious as their own had onve been, reflects an isolation from common concerns and from common images of felicity whose consequences have not yet been measured.[5]

---

[1] Eusebius, *Hist. Eccles.* VII.24.

[2] Ibid. VII.25.

[3] Eusebius, *Vita Constantini* III.15.

[4] M. I. Bakhtin, *Rabelais and his World*, tr. H. Iswolsky (M.I.T. 1968) 278.

[5] E.g., among others, D. Metlitzki, *The Matter of Araby in Medieval England* (Yale 1977) 210-219: "The Muslim Paradise as the Land of Cockayne."

Grant's paper, however, raises a more immediate issue of method, which I would like to pose in the hope of obtaining an answer from experts in New Testament studies: how do we understand the apocalyptic, millenarian and Utopian literature of ancient societies? The usual answer is that such literature represents a flight from reality, a flight that is due either to the "absurdity" of free fancy or, more respectably in Judaeo-Christian studies, to the *saeva indignatio* of a distressed group. On this view, millenarian writings are assumed to have a natural life-span: as soon as despair alleviates or as good sense prevails, they are either forgotten or are explained away by being given a "spiritual" meaning. Like Tertullian's Heavenly Jerusalem, they tend to "fade away" (p. 2) at the sunrise of peace and intelligent reflection. This certainly appears to have been their fate in the hands of the writers to whom Grant mainly refers. Yet it is extremely difficult, on this theory of "obsolescence by evaporation," to account for the continuity and stability of the interest in such matters that has preserved the manuscript tradition of this *genre* throughout the Middle Ages.[6]

Could we suggest for debate another interpretation of the function of such florid dreams? Far from erupting only at times of acute crisis, millennial dreams and apocalyptic fears formed a constant discreet lighting system for much of Christian life. Their main function was to define day-to-day reality all the more sharply by "bracketing" it between its grandiose alternatives. Like an actor caught in the pool of soft light created by the overlap of two vivid spotlights of differing color, Mediterranean men plodded through the *grauer Alltag* thankful for its lack of melodrama: even if their earth would not give its fruit "ten thousand for one" (2 Baruch 29:5), at least their one-year-old children would not "speak out with voices," their wives would not "bring forth untimely births at three or four months, and these shall live and dance," and no matter how bad things might get, at least, never "suddenly shall the sown places appear unsown, and the full storehouses shall suddenly be found empty." (4 Ezra 6:21-23). A similar deliberate heightening of the value of the concrete human condition seems to have been at work in the story of the *Odyssey*: for Odysseus slowly makes his way home to the common earth and the common pieties (linked to the common foods) of Ithaca, having passed through a series of beguiling but vaguely disturbing Utopias.[7]

I would like to follow through one aspect of the image of the two spotlights. These do not vanish as the Christian church places a distance between itself and its sectarian Jewish roots. They are still there, to cast the occasional vivid fleck of color on the actors, and in so doing, they endow with greater resonance, majesty and a sense of *la vie sérieuse* the disasters and the occasional lucky breaks of Mediterranean life. Recent sociological discussion both of "charisma" and of "liminality" would lead me to suspect

---

[6]P. Alexander, *Religious and Political History and Thought in the Byzantine Empire* (Variorum: London 1978), articles xi through xvi.

[7]P. Vidal-Naquet, "Valeurs religieuses et mythiques de la terre et du sacrifice," *l'Odysee Annales* 25 (1970) = *Le chasseur noir* (Paris 1981) 39-68.

that millennial thought cannot be easily "periodized," nor can it be dismissed (as many of the Fathers of the Church tended to do) as a stage of crude "Jewish" fantasizing, which the passing of time had disproved and the application of Hellenic good sense had rendered "merely" allegorical. Rather, it continued as a permanent form of "anti-structure," endemic in the culture and the institutions of the ancient world.[8] What changes, then, is not the judiciousness of learned clergymen faced with uneducated visions of the future, so much as their increased ability to offer and to orchestrate other forms of experience of "anti-structure." Some of these forms could be equally intense, but, mercifully for the resources of a sorely-tried society, all were less frequent and, above all, were not expected, as was the millennium, to outlast their welcome on earth.

One thing can be said with certainty of the Mediterranean and the western Near East: here was a society which firmly believed (and with every justification, given its technological incapacity) that it was pushing against the outer limits of its resources. It was a world of strictly limited goods. Little changes, in this respect, by the sixteenth century, when the same world can be studied with greater quantitative certainty. Hence the continued relevance to historians of ancient religion of the deeply humane and concrete work of Fernand Braudel.[9] As he puts it: "A double constraint has always been at the heart of Mediterranean history: poverty and the uncertainty of the morrow."[10] This is not only a world where famine is recurrent; for famine itself is merely the logical outcome, in a given region, of an unremitting general condition of shortage of natural resources.

Hence, we have a society marked by two features. The first has been exhaustively studied and evoked with tones of understandable disapproval: there is a direct and unveiled link between wealth and the power to draw to oneself, with varying degrees of unabashed brutality, a share of the limited goods of others. In the eastern Mediterranean, the fight for the control of what little agrarian surplus there was was usually at its most remorseless within range of the great towns. The victims were almost inevitably the peasantry; and the result was a chronic condition of shortage and malnutrition, always ready to tip over into famine and epidemics. If abundance existed, it could only be found among the rich and their clients in the towns.[11]

---

[8] Esp. E. Shils, *Center and Periphery* (Chicago 1975) 256-75. Shils implies the need to abandon a strict "Weberian" periodization of the history of the early church (Sohm and Harnack therein included!); Victor Turner, "Social Dramas and Stories about Them," *On Narrative*, ed. W. J. T. Mitchell (Chicago 1981) 137-64, is a recent vigorous statement of his position.

[9] F. Braudel, *The Mediterranean and the Mediterranean World in the Age of Philip II*, tr. Sian Reynolds (New York 1976) i: esp. 241-56.

[10] Ibid. 245.

[11] A. H. M. Jones, *The Later Roman Empire* (Oxford 1964) II:810-11. Cf. *Exodus R.*31, 7--cited, but misunderstood, by M. Avi-Yonah, *Geschichte der Juden im Zeitalter des Talmud* (Berlin 1963) 110, and the chilling observations of Galen cited in P. Brown, *The World of Late Antiquity* (New York 1972) 12.

The second aspect is less well-known: the pervasive linking of status and diet. Power was the power to eat. The divisions of society coincided transparently with gradations of access to foodstuffs: more food, more varied and better-prepared at the top; less food and less varied towards the bottom. "It is good for a man to dream that he is eating the kind of bread to which he is accustomed. For to a poor man, black bread is appropriate, and to a rich man, white bread."[12] As in modern Upper Egypt, meat was almost totally beyond the horizon of the villager.[13] Cooked food itself was not available to the truly poor.[14] At the top, we find poultry and game birds. These are the food of the unimaginably rich: of the impoverished rich man from Sepphoris, who ate nothing else[15]; the markets of Antioch have to stock such goods, as a sign of the superabundant wealth of the city[16]; in the Greek East, the producer of pheasants receives a Latin, Roman name, that links him to the hard eating of the most powerful group of all.[17] Squatting in the public lavatory of Justinianic Smyrna, the rich man could read the elegant verse inscriptions of Agathias: his excruciating labors are due to poultry, to fish, to carefully pounded patés and sauces; happy the honest countryman whose forced abstemiousness makes his visit prompt and painless![18] In dreams, human excrement is a sign of dishonor, but it is also the sign of the release of retained surpluses of wealth.[19] This is an age where thought about eating was, inevitably, a form of second thought about society and its blatant divisions.

How to break the iron grip of shortage? Inevitably, the best and most stunning miracles refer, not to the millennial hope of restoring the lost generosity of the earth, but to the far more difficult feat of persuading the harder hearts of men to open up: a series of miracles, that reach back into the turbulence of the Greek cities, deal with this urgent issue--how can the granaries of the rich be made to swing open?[20] Ephraem of Edessa was hailed as "a key cut by God" because he could make those heavy locks turn.[21] In this process of

---

[12] Artemidorus of Daldis, *The Interpretation of Dreams*, tr. R. White, Noyes Classical Studies (New Jersey 1975) 69.

[13] Jones, op. cit. I 446 and III 116 n. 88.

[14] E. Patlagean, *Pauvreté économique et pauvreté sociale à Byzance* (Paris 1977) 36-53. Cf. 101-12 on the illnesses related to malnutrition.

[15] *Kethuboth* 67b in H. L. Strack-P. Billerbeck, *Kommentar zum Neuen Testament aus Midrasch und Talmud* (Munich 1975) 544.

[16] Julian, *Misopogon* 350 B.C.

[17] L. Robert, *Hellenica* 11-12 (1960) 49.

[18] Agathias in *Anthologia Graeca* ix. 642-44.

[19] Artemidorus II.26, p. 106 and III.52, p. 171.

[20] R. MacMullen, *Enemies of the Roman Order* (Oxford 1966) 345 n. 20.

[21] Gregory of Nyssa: P.G. 46.837A.

persuasion, apocalyptic topics played a discreet role in molding the expectations and sensibilities of contemporaries. Lactantius' picture of the Age of Saturn in *Institutes* V.5.3 is the doublet to the headier imagery cited by Grant on page 3:

> Nor is it strange, when the barns of the righteous were
> graciously open to all; when greed did not intercept God's
> generous gifts, to make hunger and thirst widespread: but
> all enjoyed equal abundance, when those who had gave
> generously and in great supply to those who had not.

Lactantius was not read as *News from Nowhere*. At the same time as he was writing this, Saint Spyridion of Cyprus was remembered for having been in the habit of leaving his barn door open, merely nodding towards it, for any caller to go in and take his fill, either as a gift or as an interest-free loan.[22] In this way, little flecks of apocalyptic fantasy give dignity, meaning and continuity to acts of Christian charity to the village poor, such as are lovingly recorded in the lives of the saints.[23]

Failing human generosity, earth, climate and the human body itself had to be approached to yield. We should not isolate ancient men too abruptly from their environment. The "ecosystem" in which the Mediterranean peasant was trapped, his muscles and his family as his only instruments,[24] was, mercifully, not considered totally opaque or indifferent to human will. It would be very wrong to think of the miracles performed by holy men to mitigate the crushing "random oscillation of fortunes" associated with peasant life as if they were interventions

---

[22] Sozomen, *Hist. Eccles.* I.11.

[23] Compare the *Life of Symeon Stylites*, tr. F. Lent, *Jour. Am. Or. Soc.* 35 (1915) 117: "And again in the matter of the seed which he had sown, our Lord did a great miracle. For he (Symeon) allowed the gleaners and the poor in among the sheaves, and said to them, 'Let anybody take as much as they can carry.' And Our Lord sent a blessing upon it, and there came forth sixtyfold and hundredfold," with the *Infancy Gospel of Thomas* cited by Grant (Hennecke and Schneemelcher, I 396): "he brought in a hundred measures [from the one seed he, Jesus, had sown]; and he called all the poor of the village to the threshing floor and gave them the wheat."

[24] T. Shanin, *The Awkward Class* (Oxford 1972) 28: "A peasant's household is characterized by the nearly total integration of the peasant family's life with the farming enterprise," a fact not to be forgotten when considering miracles of fertility performed for village women, and such documents as Phrygian tombstones, with their couples each equipped with the tools of their labor: Elsa Gibson, *The "Christians for Christians" Inscriptions of Phrygia*, Harvard Theological Studies xxxii (1978) esp. 44.

of divine power in a neutral "nature."²⁵ Nature was not neutral. It could be
stirred to life. To bless a field, for instance, was to regain from the dead
land the "natural" fertility given to it by God on the day of its creation,
before the days of the plough and the seed-rows: Jacob of Edessa, concrete
and fastidious as ever, reports how he had seen with his own eyes virgin earth
brought up from the depth of a fifteen-cubit well--and it flowered!²⁶ This is
what the peasant families who trekked to the holy man could hope: a miracle
conceived of as the return to the earth of its "natural" abundance:

> We have been living on this plot [one such couple told
> Nicholas of Myra] for twenty years. And its yield should
> be one hundred and twenty bushel measures, and we have never
> managed to get more than twenty-five out of it. We have
> come to worship God and the holy monastery of Sion and your
> Holiness ... for we have become impoverished and have lost
> all our resources and are dying of hunger, living on that
> plot and dying of hard work, without having anything from
> which to live.²⁷

In the same manner, the air, for whose "temperate mixture" the faithful
would pray in the *Liturgy of John Chrysostom*, was not an empty space, but a
turbid zone of conflicting wills, rustling with demons and angels, and occasionally
mercifully stilled by a waft of the rich, unchanging air that clung, unrent
by the gnawing anxiety and haste of earthly seasons, around the slopes of
Paradise²⁸--a great mountain slope, somewhere in the direction of the unimaginable
lushness of the monsoon landscapes of Southern Asia and Saba, its breezes still
hanging on the spices of the East,²⁹ ringing the earth with a perfect, physical

---

[25] Shanin, op. cit. 115-15 on the overwhelming role of "crisis and strokes of luck" as determining the "random oscillation of fortunes" in a peasant society. Shanin's list is virtually reproduced by the *Life of Theodore of Sykeon* ca. 145, tr. E. Dawes and N. H. Baynes, *Three Byzantine Saints* (Oxford 1948) 151-52. See R. Browning, "The 'Low Level' Saint's Life in the Early Byzantine World," *The Byzantine Saint*, University of Birmingham 14th Spring Symposium, ed. S. Hackel, Studies Supplementary to Sobornost 5 (1981), 117-27, and P. Brown, *Society and the Holy in Late Antiquity* (Berkeley 1982) 162-63.

[26] *Jacobi Edesseni Hexaemeron*, tr. A. Vaschalde, Corpus Scriptorum Christianorum Orientalium 97: Script. Syri 48 (Louvain 1932) 103.33 ff.

[27] G. Anrich, *Hagios Nikolaos* (Berlin 1913) I:46.

[28] *Ephrém de Nisibe: Hymnes sur le Paradis* ix.13 and x.2-5, tr. R. Lavenant, Sources chrétiennes 137 (Paris 1968) 126 and 136-37; cf. Braudel, op. cit. 256: "All agricultural life, the best part of Mediterranean life, is commanded by the need for haste. Over all looms the fear of winter. ..."

[29] Ps.-Athanasius, *Ad Antiochum ducem* 47: P.G. 28.628C.

landscape, much as the vineyard-clad hills, blessed by cool upward currents, and favored by the hermits, ringed the torrid plain where Ephraem wrote his great *Hymn to Paradise*.

There was good reason for such extreme concretization. It created, again from semi-millennial materials, a kind of "moral meteorology" which gave to the little agrotowns of the eastern Mediterranean some hope of reversing the opaque hostility of the drought by reducing it to what they could hope to achieve--the sudden, penitential softening of the heart. Basil was convinced that the air would remain bound in an iron grip above Caesarea as long as the rich held on to their surpluses at the expense of the poor. In so doing, he hoped to bring to bear on the influenctial few a moral weight as heavy and as all-embracing as the burning sky.[30]

Nor would the townsman, at least, have gone through his life wholly without a touch of carefully rationed millennial joy, provided by the rich. In Stratoniceia, for instance, "the absurdities of the Land of Cockaigne," as described by Lucian (p. 14) were made available by the gymnasiarch-priest of Zeus Panamaros for twenty-two days in the year in the second and for thirty-four in the early fourth century.[31] Against a background of carefully-stated agrarian high prices, notable after notable, in the second and third centuries, pointedly broke through the restraints of economic shortage by deluging the community with water supplies, with wine, with bread, with sweetmeats, with oil and with myrrh for the women in the public baths.[32] Urban munificence in the Greco-Roman world remained tinged with strong, if transitory and carefully-staged, Utopian overtones. Nothing shows the strength of the abiding groundswell of hope for abundance than does the impenitent survival of the practices surrounding the New Year festivities of the Kalends of January. Far into the sixth century townsmen and peasants alike would pile their tables with every species of foodstuff, hoping thereby to enact on New Year's Eve the future abundance of the year.[33] Little wonder that, in Antioch, Libanius opined that if this mood were to continue, the citizens would think they were already in the Islands of the Blessed.[34]

In the light of this, it may be that one of the deepest changes of mentality associated with the rise of Christianity in the Mediterranean world is the rise to prominence of one single meal (the Eucharist), which, though heavy with associations of interpersonal bonding in a single *human* society, was

---

[30] Basil, *Hom. in tempore famis* 2 ff: P.G. 31:308D-309B.

[31] R. MacMullen, *Paganism in the Roman Empire* (Yale 1980) 46-8.

[32] *Bulletin de Correspondance Hellenique* 11 (1887) 373 and 380-81; 2 (1888) 85-6 and 101-13.

[33] M. Meslin, *La fête des Kalendes de Janvier dan l'empire romain* (Brussels 1970) 71: Jerome, *Comm. in Isaiam ad 65:11*: P.L. 24.639; Caesarius of Arles, *Sermo* 192.3: Corpus Christianorum 104, p. 781.

[34] Libanius, *Orat.* 9.10.

carefully shorn, from an early time, of any overtones of organic, non-human abundance. Previously, a widespread frame of mind had tended to take for granted the solidarity of any settled community around the rare commodities of food and relaxation, and had intended, through moments of high and leisurely eating, to shame the dull world of Nature out of its accustomed stinginess.

Everything that we know about the festivals of the Christian Church in Late Antiquity shows the resilience of the old mentality. *Lutulenta convivia* to the bishops,[35] various forms of Christian feasting continued unabated into the Middle Ages. Only a shrill elite of clerics opposed the Mediterranean urge for the banquet.[36] Such solemn eating had never been regarded by good average Christians as in any way un-Christian, although their funerary meals have often been presented as such by more squeamish modern scholars.[37] Augustine's attempt, in the 390s, to exclude an atmosphere of high carnival from the feasts of the martyrs met with only limited success.[38] Already Paulinus of Nola was letting the poor peasants have their wine and *gaudia* on Saint Felix's day;[39] and he praised a Christian senator for feeding the poor at a banquet in the basilica of Saint Peter's at Rome.[40] Gregory of Tours later devoted twenty lines to the bouquet of a wine served on the vigil of Saint Julian: "May joined October" in that exquisite potion: it is a flavor of Ephraem's still Paradise tasted, for a night, in Tours.[41]

Indeed, in the straitened Mediterranean, the kingdom of Heaven had to have something to do with food and drink. For this reason, many of the miracles of the monks can be seen as inverted miracles of abundance. For they are miracles of abstinence and of angelic food that by-pass, quite as effectively as the land of Cockaigne of Crates, the grating search for raw materials of human eating and the social constraints implied in its gathering and transformation--the fields, the irrigation, the firesides and the wives. The holy men of Syria were known as virtuoso pioneers of "alternative sources of nutrition": "At the usual hours of meals, they each took a sickle and went to the mountainside to cut some grass on the mountains, as though they were flocks in pasture."[42] At the same time, the anecdotes collected in the *Historia Monachorum* shows a

---

[35]V. Saxer, *Morts, martyrs, reliques* (Paris 1980) 100-102.

[36]P. Brown, *The Cult of the Saints* (Chicago 1980) 26-32.

[37]P. A. Fevrier, "À propos du repas funéraire: culte et sociabilité," *Cahiers archéologiques* 26 (1977) 29-45, with other articles there cited, is a vigorous rebuttal of this narrow view. MacMullen, op. cit. n. 31, pp. 36-42 describes the importance of cultic banquets *con gusto*.

[38]Saxer, op. cit. 141-47.

[39]Paulinus, *Poem* 27.542 ff.

[40]Paulinus, *Letter* 13.15.

[41]Gregory of Tours, *de virtutibus sancti Juliani* 36.

[42]Sozomen, *Hist. Eccles.* VI.32.

Nile Valley where millennial hopes continued to flicker around the new walled convents of the monks. And these hopes were about good food and good earth. Peasants blessed by Apa Coptos had the best land in Egypt (x.28-9). To show their faith in Apa Helle, peasants planted seed in sand--and it worked (xxi.16). In times of famine, the poor streamed to the monastery of Apa Apollon, believing that he and his monks regularly received food from Heaven (vii.44). Nor is this surprising: for in the early monasteries of Pachomius, his disciples remembered the good times when "We did not look like inhabitants on earth, but like men feasting in Heaven " (*Pachomii Vita Graeca Prima*, ca. 131).

Most poignant of all are the stories of food from Paradise. Monks, who reacted with horror to the illusory presence of women in their midst, warmed their hearts without the slightest inhibition on stories such as that of the strangers who had brought to Apa Apollo "fruit from Paradise, grapes, pomegranates, figs, nuts, and all obtained out of season, honeycombs, a jug of fresh milk, enormous dates and some white bread, still warm " (vii.40). Apa Macarius the Egyptian, the Odysseus of the Desert Fathers, "traversing the desert as though it were the sea," once found his way, far to the West, to the magic garden which Jannes and Mambres had built for Pharaoh in imitation of the luxuriance of Paradise. He carefully marked the way to this Lost World with palm leaves, so as to lead his fellows back to its "sweet delights." The demons removed the trail, and our Odysseus settled back in his Ithaca--a man among men, tied to the discipline of the cell and the perpetual mortgage of the belly (xxi.5-7). These are plainly the musings of men for whom the abundance of God's Paradise had not tastefully faded away.

In a few remarks, Origen indicates the parting of the ways in Christianity. He once committed himself to what he knew were "dangerous words" on a "useful error": "Certain Christians practice sexual abstinence and celibacy, while others never remarry, because they think that he who is married or who remarries is damned."[43] They were wrong, of course; but for Origen it was a mistake in the right direction. What was truly disruptive for the church, he felt, was a widespread belief in the physical delight of the millennium: "Pray to God to save us from such teachers."[44]

By and large, Origen's prayers came to be answered. A Christian church, patronized largely by the well-fed and increasingly led by austere men such as himself, whose restricted diet was the result of choice and not of necessity, found itself, in the next centuries, increasingly tempted to treat sexuality (a drive which frequently assumes leisure and regular eating habits), rather than greed and greed's dark shadow in a world of limited resources and famine, as the most abiding and disquieting symptom of the fraility of the human condition. Maybe the time has come to look again at the seemingly absurd dreams of abundance of ancient Mediterranean men, to find, through their concerns, one way, at least, to more humane and more commonsensical objects of anxiety.

---

[43] Origen, *Hom. in Jerem.* 20.4 (G.C.S. III.183) cited in H. Crouzel, *Virginité et Mariage selon Origene* (Paris 1963) 92.

[44] Origen, *Hom. in Ezech.* 3. 3 and 6 (G.C.S. VII 350 and 354) in Crouzel, op. cit., 130.

Response by K. M. Irwin, Ph.D. Student
Graduate Theological Union, Berkeley

Using the visual art of the Early Church as evidence for any thesis must be done with caution, as most of the examples before the fifth century are from the Roman catacombs--frescoes and sculptured tombs--and this funerary context imposes a limit on the range of interpretations for individual works.

In dealing with the Christian art of late antiquity, it is difficult to arrive at criteria that would distinguish between a literal and a spiritual interpretation of miraculous feedings. There does seem to be a shift from what Grabar calls "sign-image"[1] to a narrative image. In frescoes of the third and fourth centuries in the catacombs of both Callistus[2] and Peter and Marcellinus we find meal scenes which have been interpreted as one (or more) of the following: (1) eucharistic ceremony, (2) agape, (3) refrigerium or funeral banquet, (4) messianic meal, or (5) feeding miracle story. By the sixth century, specific gospel stories that can be identified as the Last Supper,[3] the Wedding at Cana,[4] or the Multiplication of the Loaves and Fishes[5] are more common.

Perhaps this shift from the sumbolic to the narrative can be seen as an evolution of images from a spiritual interpretation to a literal one if we equate the polyvalent image with the spiritual and the narrative or descriptive image with the literal interpretation.

Although fish may not be as important as bread and wine, or whether two fish can be interpreted as food for the messianic age,[6] which Professor Grant seems to doubt, the many images of two fish found in the visual art of these times cannot be dismissed.[7]

The importance of the Dionysus "wine miracle" was not lost on the early Church in the East, it seems, as there was an early association of the Cana story with the liturgy for the feast of the Epiphany on January 6.

---

[1] A. Grabar, *Christian Iconography; A Study of Its Origins* (Princeton 1968).

[2] Figure 1 shows a typical meal scene from Callistus, the Sacrament Chapel.

[3] Figure 2, mosaic from S. Apollinare Nuovo, Ravenna, ca. 525. There are no known Last Supper scenes in catacomb or sarcophagus art.

[4] Two frescoes from Peter and Marcellinus are known to be pre-fourth century.

[5] Several fourth century tomb sculptures. The Cana story and Multiplication of the Loaves is combined on a panel from the doors of S. Sabina, ca. 430, with seven water jars, and seven baskets.

[6] Richard Hiers and Charles Kennedy, "Bread and Fish Eucharist in the Gospels and Early Christian Art," *Perspectives in Religious Studies* 3 (Spring 1976) 20-47.

[7] See figures 1 through 6 for examples. Hiers and Kennedy's list: pp. 21-23.

A symbol concerned with the Golden Age that seems to have been important in both pagan and Christian art is that of the phoenix.[8] The return to the Golden Age, seen in the appearance of a new ruler and the beginning of a new era, was heralded by the phoenix,[9] the symbol of renewal for both pagans and Christians.[10] The abode of the phoenix was seen to be the Isles of the Blessed where the Golden Age persists, or in Paradise.[11] An often repeated image system can be seen in the apse mosaic of SS. Cosmas e Damiano, Rome, A.D. 526-30, where the phoenix with its seven-rayed halo signals the arrival of Christ coming "on the clouds."[12]

What is the real value in choosing between a literal and a spiritual interpretation of the feeding miracles? Preserving the tension between the real and the symbolic is vital, it seems to me. Should we limit the understanding of these stories by insisting on a single theory of interpretation?

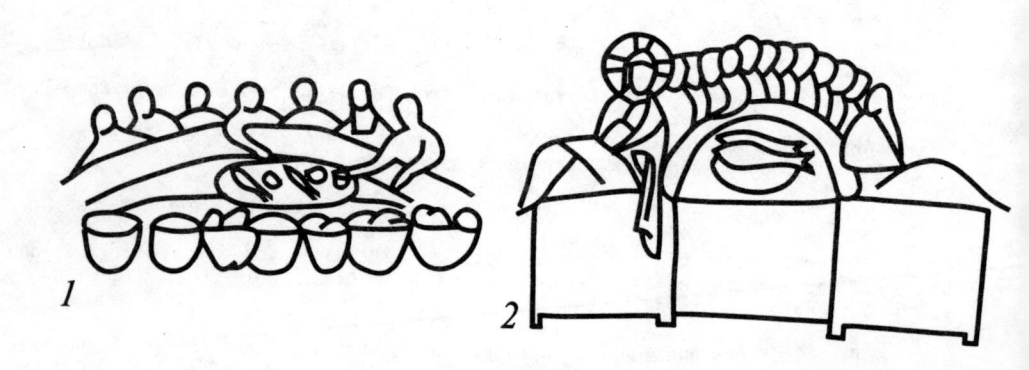

---

[8] Figure 7, detail of a floor mosaic in a Roman villa near Piazza Amerina, Sicily.

[9] R. van den Broek, *The Myth of the Phoenix According to Classical and Early Christian Tradition* (Leiden 1972), 105.

[10] Ibid. p. 113.

[11] Ibid. p. 419.

[12] Figure 8.

3

4

5

6

7

8

Response by Irene Lawrence, Lecturer in Religious Studies
University of California, Davis

Fish, Figs, Grapes, and Barley Grow

Professor Grant has given us a multi-faceted and entertaining paper, which covers more geographic and symbolic territory than I am competent to deal with. Therefore, I will discuss only a few issues, unrelated to each other, raised by the paper.

First, there is the matter of the cursing of the fig tree (pp. 5-6). It is not one of the miracles of "feeding, of the multiplication of bread and wine, and of miraculous fertility" (p. 1), but is, rather, a miracle of "anti-fertility," the only one that occurs to me, at least in the Synoptic Gospels. But since there are so many Biblical precedents linking fig trees with vines, speaking of vines (as on p. 4) almost automatically leads to speaking of fig trees. Since these Old Testament associations would be strong in the minds of the Gospel writers and early Christian interpreters, it may be worthwhile to review them here. Figs and vines were often cultivated together; their prosperity is a symbol of peace and plenty in the land.[1] Similarly, the lack of or destruction of the vine and the fig tree means the absence or end of prosperity and peace.[2] I found two other passages that associate vines and figs with each other, Hos. 9:10 and Jer. 8:13; both of these identify Israel in some way with the vine and the fig tree, and in both the context is Israel's unfaithfulness--what my annotated RSV rather quaintly calls "Israel's incredible indifference" to God's law.[3] In Hosea, the grapes and figs represent Israel of old, fruitful in contrast to its present state:

> Like grapes in the wilderness,
>   I found Israel.
> Like the first fruits on the fig tree,
>   in its first season,
>   I found Israel.   (Hos. 9:10)

And in Jeremiah, the fruitlessness of vine and fig tree are identified with contemporary Israel:

---

[1] E.g., Num. 13:23, It. 8:8, 1 Kg. 4:25, 2 Kg. 18:31-Is. 36:16 (here the offerer of the peace and plenty is the King of Assyria--until the deportation, after which there will be even more peace and plenty), S. of S. 2:13, Jl. 2:22, Mic. 4:4, Hag. 2:19, Zech. 3:10, and even 1 Macc. 14:12.

[2] Num. 20:5, Ps. 105:33, Is. 34:4, Jer. 5:17, Hos. 2:12, Jl. 1:7, 12, and Hab. 3:17. Several other passages link the prosperity of the vine alone to that of Israel.

[3] *The New Oxford Annotated Bible with the Apocrypha*, Expanded Edition, RSV (Oxford University Press 1977), p. 921.

> When I would gather them, says the LORD,
>   there are no grapes on the vine,
>   nor figs on the fig tree;
> Even the leaves are withered,
>   and what I gave them has passed
>   away from them.   (Jer. 8:13)

I am not aware of other passages in which Israel is identified with a fig tree,[4] but identification with a vine seems much more common, occuring independently of the fig tree in several other places,[5] including the *locus classicus*, Is. 5:1-7.

If we change "LORD" in the Jeremiah passage to "Lord", and then have Jesus act out the fig tree part instead of telling it as a parable, we have the core of Mark 11:12-14 and 20-21. That Mark understands the story as symbolic of Israel is shown by its placement around the cleansing of the temple. Further, after the brief discussions on faith and authority which follow (Mark 11:20-33), we have the vine motif picked up and used in the extended parable of the wicked tenants, where now the vineyard is unfruitful for its owner because of the wickedness of its tenants. I am not knowledgeable about the history of Biblical interpretation, but I suspect that the identification of Israel with vine and fig tree in passages like these was common, even with different methods of interpretation--apocalyptic, allegorical, literal, or combined. At least two interpreters, Matthew and Luke, took the identification for granted when they reworked Mark's material for their own purposes;[6] Luke even "replaced this story with a parable" (p. 5), making the identification even clearer.

Second, Professor Grant discusses (pp. 2-3) the continuation of apocalyptic eschatology in the face of increasing non-apocalyptic spirituality from the second century on. He provides quotations which, in their self-conscious and rather defensive insistence on apocalyptic eschatology, could be paralleled by many twentieth-century "orthodox" Christians who sincerely hold, for example, that the so-called "Second Coming," in all its apocalyptic trappings, is a necessary part of the Christian faith. In this sense, certainly "apocalyptic eschatology did not fade away in the second century" (p. 2)--or, for that matter, in the twentieth.

---

[4] Is. 28:4 identifies the "proud crown of the drunkards of Ephraim" with "a first-ripe fig before the summer"; it gets eaten up immediately. Figs, not trees, in Jer. 24:1-10, symbolize those who undergo exile in Babylon (good figs) and those who remain behind in Jerusalem (bad figs); similarly, in Jer. 29:17 those who did not go into exile are "vile figs which are so bad they cannot be eaten." And, although it is not about Israel, it may be appropriate to mention Nah. 3:12, which calls Nineveh's fortresses "fig trees with first-ripe figs" that practically drop into the eaters' mouths.

[5] For example, Ps. 80:8-15, Hos. 14:7, Jer. 2:21, possibly Jer. 6:9, and Ezek. 15:6, 17:6-8, 19:10-14.

[6] I am assuming, of course, Marcan priority here.

But I wonder whether this self-conscious apocalyptic thinking functions for interpretation in the same way as the unexamined and therefore unified apocalyptic world view of the earlier writers. We seem to have moved from Mk. 1:15, "the time is fulfilled, and the reign of God is at hand," to something more like Lewis Carroll (to bring in yet another agricultural entity, suggested by Professor Grant's subtitles), "The rule is, jam to-morrow, and jam yesterday--but never jam today." From the unquestioning belief that God is about to bring about a new order now, apocalyptic thought moved from the here and now to the distant future, and perhaps the distant past. In terms of agricultural expectations, the distant future should be at least as good as the distant past, Eden; the curse pronounced at the expulsion (Gen. 3:14-19) will no longer hold. The curse describes the current situation:

> cursed is the ground because of you;
> in toil you shall eat of it all the
> days of your life;
> ...
> In the sweat of your face
> you shall eat bread .... (Gen. 3:17, 19)

But in the future it will be different. (Incidently, this is the man's part of the curse, spoken to Adam. I do not have any snakes' or women's speculations as to what the apocalyptic future holds for them.)

Also, I think the change in what apocalyptic meant affected the understanding of "literal" (or in its usual twentieth-century form, "historical") and "non-literal" interpretation. Apocalyptic seems to have changed to a category under literal, and may have influenced the mental split between "literal" and other interpretation that plagues the church even today. It is under this mentality that inconsistencies such as Jesus cursing the fig tree for barrenness when it was not the season for figs become problems. (And that apparently was a problem for both Matthew, who eliminated the remark about the season, and Luke, who also eliminated it from his much changed version.) Even Origen, who apparently was perfectly willing to abandon the literal meaning of any given text, used any "oddity" in the literal meaning (such as Jesus' irresponsible behavior about the fig tree[7]) to signal the need for abandoning it. So even for a thoroughgoing allegorist like Origen, the literal meaning has an independence and a primacy that I am not sure it would have had if consistent apocalypticism still held sway.

Third, I am curious about the "Possible Pagan Frameworks" and parallels suggested by Professor Grant (pp. 12-15). I suppose that some of the Christian stories, when taken out of context, might sound like some of these entertaining Land of Cockaigne stories, much as today we might mentally connect them with various Paul Bunyan stories or the Big Rock Candy Mountain, which has cigarette trees and rock 'n' rye springs, where "lovely streams of alcohol come trickling down the rocks," and "there's a lake of stew and good home brew." But the

---

[7]I do not know whether Origen in fact ever discusses this particular example.

resemblance seems to end there. Leaving the parodies out, the serious pictures are of a happy and productive nature, where the rules are merely a little different from those around us. These lands are distant, but they are basically part of our own world. Miraculous feedings in the New Testament belong to the new world that God is bringing (or will bring) about. Any resemblance, then, is only on the surface.

Finally, I had some speculations about fish, not to be taken very seriously. Professor Grant rightly remarks that "it cannot be said that fish are as significant as bread and wine in the life of the church militant or at rest" (p. 10). And yet they are "multiplied without emphasis" (p. 10) in all versions of the feedings of the Four and Five Thousand, and fish are involved in resurrection appearances in both Luke 24:36-43 (where Jesus eats a piece of broiled fish) and John 21:1-14, which Professor Grant mentions. The bread in all these stories is traditionally associated with the bread of the Eucharist, and Luke 24:28-35, which immediately precedes the "fish story" mentioned above, is the famous "Road to Emmaus" story which ends "he was known to them in the breaking of the bread." Yet with all these Biblical suggestions, the church apparently did not sacramentalize the sharing of fish.[8] There are probably sound practical reasons involved; it is difficult enought to keep wine and bread fresh. On this assumption, the liturgical practice (fishless) of the church would have influenced the traditions of the Last Supper.

---

[8] I have a vague idea that fish appeared frequently in early Christian art, but if so I do not know whether they represented stories such as these or whether they were influenced by the acronym ΙΧΘΥΣ.

Response by Mary Rosenthal Lefkowitz, Andrew W. Mellon Professor in Humanities
Wellesley College

In his paper "The Problem of Miraculous Feedings in the Graeco-Roman Period," Professor Grant implies that pagans shared with Christians a strong and literal belief in a time of abundance. But I think it more likely that educated pagans would have regarded the notion of miracle feedings as absurd. In Greco-Roman mythology, the Golden Age and Isles of the Blessed are always described as remote in time and space, accessible only to extraordinary men like heroes, or to persons who have undergone some special process of initiation (such as the Eleusinian mysteries) or purification (Orphism); but the miracle feedings of the New Testament take place in familiar settings, and in a specified historical period.

Accounts of the Golden Age were intended primarily as paradigms. In Hesiod's *Works and Days*, the Golden Age represents the ideal from which men have fallen as a result of their immorality and belligerence. Vergil's extravagant vision of the coming age in *Eclogue* 4 was inspired by a desire to escape from the harsh realities of civil war; so was Horace's description in *Epode* 16 of life in the Blessed Fields. No one would have believed that these were "relatively serious pictures," meant to be taken literally. They were understood by their authors and audiences to be utopias.[1]

It seems to me that in the *True History* (2.13), Lucian has in mind not so much the ideal fertility of Hesiod's Golden Age or the utopian island of Phaeacia (*Odyssey* 7.112) as the specific fantastic numbers of Judeo-Christian apocalypse and miracle stories. In the *Revelation to John* (22:2), the tree of life bears twelve harvests in the year, one harvest per month; in the Elysian Fields of Lucian's *True History*, "there are twelve vintages in the year, with the grapes ripening every month."[2]

A Jew like Philo or a Christian like Lactantius could reasonably claim that the Apocalypse represented a second Golden Age; whether they realized it or not, from the earliest times pagan mythology had incorporated materials from the Near East--for example, the Succession Myth in Hesiod's *theogony* or the *Myth of Ages* (including the Golden Age) in the *Works and Days*.[3] The Sibylline Oracles that Vergil mentions in *Eclogue* 4:4 included material from oriental--indeed Jewish--apocalyptic.[4] Lucian knew about Christian beliefs and certainly had opportunity to see or hear specific sacred texts. But in the writings of educated pagans the fervent hopes of the Hebrew prophets became

---

[1] E. Gabba, *JRS* 71 (1981) 59.

[2] Cf. F. G. Allinson, *Lucian: Selected Writings* (Boston 1905) 56.

[3] See esp. M. L. West, *Hesiod: Theogony* (Oxford 1966) 18 ff.; Hesiod: *Works and Days* (Oxford 1978) 172 ff.

[4] R. Coleman, *Vergil: Eclogues* (Cambridge 1977) 130.

rhetorical illustrations and entertaining fantasy. For them the gods, despite all the reverence that their power and beauty demanded, remained as remote from men and as inaccessible as the Elysian Fields. In *Aeneid* 6, Aeneas visits the Elysian Fields and learns of the glorious future of Rome; but Vergil has him leave the Lower World through the gate of False Dreams.[5]

---

[5] W. Clausen, "An Interpretation of the *Aeneid*," in *Virgil*, ed. S. Commager (Englewood Cliffs, N.J. 1966) 87-88; cf. R. G. Austin, *Aeneidos Liber Sextus* (Oxford 1977) 276.

Response by Susan Marie Praeder, Assistant Professor of Theology
Boston College

Classification of Miracle Stories and Spiritual Interpretation of the New Testament[1]

In the opening paragraph of his paper Professor Grant refers to two problems which are part of the critical study of the miracle stories of antiquity: the classification of miraculous feedings and the interpretation of miraculous feedings in relation to the laws of nature and spiritual reality. I agree with his implied criticism of the classification "nature miracle" (p. 1) as a conglomeration of rescues, provisions, punishments, and revelations.[2] But I disagree that the passages that he later cites from classical, scriptural, patristic, and other writings "constitute a special class" (p. 1) of miracles of feeding, food and drink, and fertility. Only a few of the passages contain miracles, and even these few passages represent several types of miracle stories. Professor Grant approaches the problem of interpretation by assembling evidence for the limits of agricultural, horticultural, and viticultural reality and for spiritual explication of the New Testament in patristic exegesis. Without questioning the accuracy or the importance of Professor Grant's evidence, I cannot accept his agricultural interpretation of the parable of the sower in Mark 4:3-8 or his treatment of the history of the tradition and interpretation of the cursing and withering of the fig tree in Mark 11:12-14, 20-21 as the spiritualization of an embarrassingly incredible story.

Classification of Miracle Stories

The passages cited by Professor Grant include miracle stories which seem to suspend the laws of nature and prophecies and reminiscences of seemingly remarkable occurrences which nevertheless conform to the laws of nature of other times and places. Among the miracle stories are two from the Old Testament, the provision of the manna in Exodus 16 and the sufficiency of the loaves in 2 Kings 4; ten from the New Testament, the six multiplications of loaves and fishes in Matthew 14 and 15, Mark 6 and 8, Luke 9, and John 6, the two catches of fish in Luke 5 and John 21, the cursing and withering of the fig tree in Mark 11, and the transformation of water into wine in John 2; two from Christian apocrypha, the sowing of grain in the *Infancy Gospel of Thomas* 12 and the sufficiency of the loaves in the *Acts of John* 93; and the numerous reports of

---

[1] My response to Professor Grant's paper reflects two areas of my research interest. To the classification of miracle stories I will contribute some of what I have learned as the coordinator for Christian texts for the Society of Biblical Literature Miracle Stories Work Group. Through my application of narrative analysis and interpretation to the New Testament I have come to regard "spiritual interpretation" as a natural and necessary result of reading the New Testament.

[2] For the classification "nature miracle," see Rudolf Bultmann, *The History of the Synoptic Tradition* (1968) 215-18.

rivers of wine and the provision of wine in Greco-Roman reference works. As miracle stories these passages relate events of the past which not only bent or broke the laws of nature of the "then and there" of the participants but also bend and break the laws of nature of the "here and now" of the readers/hearers.[3]

Except for the cursing and withering of the fig tree, all the miracle stories involve the provision of food, fish, or wine. Even so, the value of their classification as a special class of "provision miracles" is questionable, especially in view of the various types of provisions.[4] For example, of the gospel miracles only the multiplications of the loaves and fishes seem to constitute a special class of miraculous feedings. The catches of fish are fishing miracles, not feeding miracles, and the transformation of the water into wine is a miracle of production, not of satiation.

Although the prophecies in the sections "Bread Tomorrow" and "Wine Tomorrow" and the descriptions of the Golden Age and the Blessed Isles in "Possible Pagan Frameworks" break the laws of nature of the here and now, they conform to the laws of nature of the times and places of their occurrence. The prophecies refer to the eschatological age, when remarkable yields of bread and wine will be the agricultural and viticultural rules.[5] In the Golden Age leisure and luxury extraordinary in the Iron Age were the ordinary "works and days" of the human race. The laws of nature operative in the Blessed Isles are obviously "not of this world."

Of course, the fact that the accounts of the Golden Age and the Blessed Isles are not miraculous need not rule out the possibility of their influence on the composition or interpretation of miracle stories in antiquity. But Professor Grant's paper offers evidence to the contrary. The miracle stories are local in extent and temporary in effect; they do not transform the face of the earth. Typically, they involve a miracle worker or evince divine interest in a worshiping community or the human community. In contrast, the wonders of the Golden Age and the Blessed Isles are general, self-renewing and long-lasting, if not permanent. Although the gods may preside over the god-beloved in such times and places, nature itself is the good provider.

---

[3] Also of note is that the miralces cited by Professor Grant tend to be stories. The nonmiraculous occurrences are often reported in summary lists.

[4] For the classification *Geschenkwunder*, see Gerd Theissen, *Urchristliche Wundergeschichten: Ein Beitrag zur formgeschichtlichen Erforschung der synoptischen Evangelien* (1974) 111-14.

[5] Even when prophecies refer to miraculous events, they cannot be regarded as reports of miracles because the events have not yet occurred in real or imaginary time.

Spiritual Interpretation of the New Testament

Of the patristic interpretations of the parable of the sower, Professor Grant states, "None of this has anything to do with the agricultural setting of the parable" (p. 8). Although the parable has an agricultural setting and the allegorical identifications of Irenaeus and Origen are far-fetched, the parable is certainly to be understood spiritually rather than agriculturally. I therefore find Professor Grant's effort to establish the exceptional nature of thirtyfold, sixtyfold, and hundredfold yields of wheat largely irrelevant to the interpretation of the parable. The conclusion of the parable concerns the returns of faith; it has nothing to do with "a yearning for a rate of growth beyond what was thought possible" (p. 7).

The spiritual interpretations of Irenaeus and Origen are not simply to be assigned to the excesses of patristic exegesis. The very nature of parables as "stories about something" and of the parables of Jesus as communications of the secrets of the kingdom of God invites spiritual interpretations by their readers/hearers. The Gospel of Mark suggests that spiritual interpretation of the parable of the sower is almost as old as the parable itself. The parable in Mark 4:3-8 is accompanied by a spiritual interpretation of the parable in Mark 4:13-20. According to the interpretation attributed by Mark to Jesus, the seed is the word, the four sowings are hearings of the word, and the fates of the seeds are the faith-lives of the hearers. Two questions introduce the interpretation of this first in a series of parables, "You don't understand this parable? Then how will you understand all the parables?" Indeed, as the parable of the sower seems to be a parable about parabling, thus the interpretation of the parable of the sower offers a paradigm for parable interpretation.

Professor Grant reconstructs the history of the tradition of the cursing and withering of the fig tree as a redactional process of removal of "the embarrassing features" of the story. In the history of interpretation the barrenness of the fig tree in the eschatological season is supposed to have been transformed into an allegory of the hard-heartedness of the people of Israel. In regard to the history of tradition, there is no evidence that the saying about the fig tree in Mark 13:28 moderates the cursing story or that the parable of the fig tree in Luke 13:6-9 replaced the Markan miracle story.[6] Moreover, already in Mark the cursing and withering of the fig tree admits of application to the fate of Jewish worship. The two parts of the story, Mark 11:12-14 and Mark 11:20-21, frame the story of the cleansing of the temple in Mark 11:15-19. Thus, Mark 11:12-21 is an instance of Markan "intercalation," and the story of the fig tree is a commentary on the proceedings in the temple at Jerusalem.[7] Several interpretations are possible. Either the withering of

---

[6] For the view that the miracle story is the adaptation of a saying or parable, see the references in R. Bultmann, *Synoptic Tradition*, 425, n. 18.

[7] For a list of Markan intercalations, see John R. Donahue, *Are You the Christ? The Trial Narrative in the Gospel of Mark* (1973) 42, n. 2. For interpretation of Mark 11:12-21, see D. E. Nineham, *Saint Mark* (1977) 298-99.

the fig tree is as unnatural as the rendering of a house if prayer into a
den of thieves or the fate of the fig tree signals the end of the temple or
the end of the efficacy of temple worship.

MINUTES OF THE COLLOQUY OF 14 MARCH 1982

List of Participants

Professor at the *University of Chicago*
    Robert M. Grant *(New Testament and Early Christianity)*

Professors at the *University of California, Berkeley*
    William S. Anderson *(Classics)*
    Baruch M. Bokser *(Near Eastern Studies)*
    Julian Boyd *(English)*
    Peter Brown *(Classics and History)*
    Erich Gruen *(History)*
    Charles E. Murgia *(Classics)*
    Danuta Shanzer *(Classics)*
    Wayne Shumaker *(English, Emeritus)*

Professors at the *Graduate Theological Union*
    Michael B. Aune *(Liturgics)*
    Michael L. Cook *(Systematic Theology)*
    Robert B. Coote *(Old Testament)*
    John R. Donahue *(New Testament)*
    Sherman E. Johnson *(Dean Emeritus, CDSP)*
    Anitra B. Kolenkow *(Visiting Scholar, DSPT)*
    Thomas W. Leahy *(Biblical Studies)*
    Daniel Matt *(Judaic Studies)*
    Martha Stortz *(Historical Theology and Ethics)*
    David Winston *(Hellenistic and Judaic Studies)*
    Antoinette Wire *(New Testament)*
    John H. Wright *(Systematic Theology)*
    Wilhelm Wuellner *(New Testament)*

Professor at *Pacific Union College*
    Fred Veltman *(New Testament)*

Professor at the *University of California, Davis*
    Irene Lawrence *(Lecturer, Religious Studies)*

Professors at the *University of San Francisco*
    Marvin Brown *(College of Professional Studies)*
    John H. Elliott *(Exegetical Theology)*

Guests
    David L. Bartlett *(Lakeshore Baptist Church)*
    Sharon Boucher *(CHS Business Manager)*
    Jon F. Dechow
    Aidan A. Kelly *(Holy Family College)*
    Chris Salak

Students
    K. M. Irwin
    Robert Maldonado
    Jef Van Gerwen
    Victor Yoon

MINUTES OF THE COLLOQUY OF 14 MARCH 1982

THE DISCUSSION

Summarized by Irene Lawrence

Grant: In this, as in most of my theological studies, I have been looking for tangible, concrete, reality. It started when I was confirmed at the age of twelve and received my first communion, causing some disconcertment to my mother because I said, "This looks like fish food." That wafer is a symbol of the *un*reality of life even in the church, which I take to be a fairly tangible reality. So much of my work has been to fight what Whitehead should have called "misplaced spiritualization."

My teacher, Arthur Darby Nock, criticized Bultmann for starting with tangible people talking about tangible things but moving into the world of *Geistesgeschichte* and disappearing. Thus my comments a few years ago to this group on the political functions of a bishop like Cyprian* were based not on ancient political ideas but on thirty years of experience of academic and other politics in Chicago.[1] This sort of approach is enormously neglected by professional scholars of all sorts.

In this paper I am trying to look at some of the peculiar features of early Christianty, but is the categorization that important? "Utopian," "eschatological," appear in the possible discussion questions; the terms may be helpful academically but surely have no innate significance. Is it not more important to come in contact with the material and let it talk to us? Classification and analysis can both be called academic diseases.

In her response, Professor Praeder discussed the "spiritual" quality of these miracle stories; I think that would depend on the context of the interpretation. They were not so understood by most readers.[2] And one should add the countless similar miracle stories in the *Acta Sanctorum*, which I should have mentioned. *White Magic: An Introduction to the Folklore of Christian Legend* by C. Grant Loomis[3] has special sections on bread, fish, wine, etc., and their marvelous multiplication by the saints. Occasionally something would go slightly wrong, and they would inadvertently multiply beer instead of wine.

I certainly do not disagree with anything in K. Irwin's response. The phoenix is certainly worth discussing, but since it is not eaten, it does not provide a parallel in this context. The number of early Christians who reject the

---

*[Editor's note: See Colloquy 35, 25 February 1979]

[1] See the article on Ephesus by Anna Crabba in *JTS* 32 (1981), 369-400.

[2] Instances occur in Porphyry's criticism of water into wine and John Chrysostom's defence of it.

[3] Medieval Academy, 1948.

story of the phoenix is also worth noting; there were Theophilus and Clement, and even Origen is reluctant to discuss it.

Professor Lawrence calls the fig tree a miracle of anti-fertility; I would call it failed fertility, but this does make it all the more significant. I welcome a quotation from Lewis Carroll as a token that levity is an important part of *Wissenschaft*.

Professor Lefkowitz says that pagan stories were different from Christian ones. I wonder if we can be so certain that a pagan would not treat a Golden Age story as paradigmatic. Something like a tradition turns up in the materials given by Lovejoy and Boas.[4]

As for Professor Brown's charming and incisive comments, I wish I had thought of relating Constantine's banquet (p. 16) to this theme. I have tried to suggest that despair does not produce apocalyptic dreams. Things do not happen for just one cause, and I do not now think that apocalyptic or gnostic dreams mirror a social reality. Something external may trigger the dream, but it mirrors something going on inside the apocalyptic thinker's psyche. I like the idea of "bracketing" (p. 17).

We find in Josephus that the productivity of Galilee was really startling during this period, and so real hunger is not the immediate issue. Apocalyptic therefore may be one more testimony to human greed, at least the greed of those who own the means of production. "The victims were almost inevitably the peasantry" (p. 18). Although I am definitely not a Marxist, a Marxist analysis can draw attention to industrial and agricultural realities in a way that is very salutary for people who spend all their time thinking.[5]

Over a quarter of a century Origen vigorously rejected the literal interpretation of Biblical promises, from *De principiis* ii.11 through the Canticles commentary (Prol., p. 66 Baehrens) to *Matt. comm.* xvii.35 (p. 699 Klostermann). In *Princ.* ii.11.2 he insisted that the literalists would not have the assistance of various laborers to provide the materials of food and drink, "servants of their pleasures." Actually Isaiah had said (65:18-22) in a passage cited by Irenaeus (v.34.4) as meant literally (v.35.1), that "they will plant vines and eat the fruit themselves."

I share Professor Brown's interest in the contrast of Christianity's picture of life in heaven with Islam's exuberance. How and why Christianity developed such an emphasis on asceticism is not clear. It is sometimes attributed to Jewish influence, but there is conflicting evidence.

I would like to add one more thing. There is something like an Epicurean

---

[4]A. O. Lovejoy & G. Boas, *Primitivism and Related Ideas in Antiquity* (New York 1965).

[5]In spite of some exaggerations, we all have much to learn from G. E. M. de Ste. Croix, *The Class Struggle in the Ancient Greek World*.

eschatology in a new fragment of Diogenes of Oenoanda.[6] The highly probable translation runs like this: "Then truly the life of the gods will pass to men. For all things will be full of justice and mutual love, and there will be no need of fortifications or laws and all the things which we contrive on account of one another. And with regard to the necessaries derived from agriculture, as we shall have no [farm-laborers--for indeed we shall all plough and dig and mind flocks and divert rivers and watch. . .---. . .And such activities will interrupt the continuous study of philosophy for needful purposes; for the farming operations will provide us with the things which our nature wants.] (There are fragmentary clues to the direction of the thought within the brackets.) Here in the probably this-worldly future the wise continue to work and obtain a modest living without fantastic productivity.

M. Brown: Here are the suggested discussion questions.

1. What is the most adequate classification or genre identification of the many texts of nourishment presented by Prof. Grant and the respondants?

    a. What criteria do we employ?
       1. social-economic
       2. literary traditions
       3. ecological vs. ideological
       4. apocalyptic vs. utopian
       5. liturgical/social
       6. other
    b. What do these various texts have in common?
       1. common identity "only on the surface."
       2. belong to Mediterranean "dream of abundance."
       3. other

2. If we can approach the uses of the "dream of abundance" as a history of interpretation or "reception history," then what do the changes in the use of the "dream of abundance" tell us about Hellenistic hermeneutics?

Our first suggested question looks at the issue of classification or genre identification; the criteria in a. 1-6 are simply key terms taken from the responses, meant to be reminders of the options, not a list that must be dealt with in sequence. Professor Grant has raised a version of b: whether these texts have anything in common, and whether it is important to ask that question. The second question, of more interest to me at least, is whether there is a set of hermeneutical practices there that might help us understand Hellenistic hermeneutics as part of the history of hermeneutics. In a sense, the first question is a synchronic question, the second is diachronic.

Elliott: A question about these two questions: do they include what Professor Grant wants us to consider, the correlation between the material and social

---

[6]M. F. Smith, "Thirteen New Fragments of D. of O," *Denkschr. Oesterr. Akad. der Wiss., Philo.-hist. Kl.*, 117, 1974, pp. 21-25: new fragment 21.

setting and the ideological formulation and interpretation? If not, could we add that correlation to the list of questions?

Dechow: Before we begin the list, I would like to ask about the title of the paper itself: "The Problem of Miraculous Feedings in the Graeco-Roman Period." I did not find a clear definition of the "problem" in the paper. What are the problems?

Grant: This was my second choice for a title; in a letter dated 3 December 1980, Professor Edward Hobbs said, "We prefer 'The Problem of Miraculous Feedings. . . .'" My own choice for the title, which he rejected firmly, was "Pie on Earth or in the Sky." That was what was in my mind. I probably chose "Problem" because the word "hermeneutics" came up so much, but now I think "Credibility" or "Practicability" or "Desirability" would have been more suitable. How about: "Do Stories of Miraculous Feedings Answer Any Substantial Problems in the Graeco-Roman World?"

Dechow: But you dealt with the tendency to millenialism and literalism, and Professor Lefkowitz questioned whether intelligent pagans would be bothered with this at all.

Grant: The question is not set correctly, and therefore cannot be answered at all. We do not know what one intelligent pagan would think as compared to another; a great deal would depend on how they were brought up. We tend to discuss all these questions in terms of categories, which do not help.

Dechow: Both Christian and pagan are dealing with mythological and miraculous materials in their own traditions--even Plato. So we must be selective.

Elliott: My first reaction was to notice the affinity between some of these stories of antiquity and things like "A chicken in every pot" or supply-side economics which talk about material improvement. Clearly many intelligent people have believed such things. Therefore it seems wrong to ask whether these things are credible. Rather, we should ask who would formulate them and for what end.

Grant: That is very good. About ten years ago people were concerned with plans for all the leisure time to be provided by technology. Perhaps not having to do anything is the real dream.

Winston: There is a hint of the social context of the Cockaigne vision in Pherecrates' play *Metaleis*, the Miners. The mine shaft caves in, and the miners fall into the underworld, where these classic have-nots find all the abundance of the land of Cockaigne. It's the same vision as in the German Schlaraffenland where the geese fly into one's mouth self-roasted. There is a famous English poem of Cockaigne, dated in the early fourteenth century.

P. Brown: It is a world where every prospect pleases and only man is vile. There is a deep pessism about human nature which can only be overcome by a miraculous, quasi-technological improvement in the environment, so you do not have to compensate by fighting your neighbor for your little patch of land. Perhaps one of the points about nature miracles is not whether they happen or not, but that they deliberately happen outside the sphere of the human. That is, you know you cannot alter the landlords or the peasants, but you might be able to coax the earth into being a little less difficult. Perhaps the history of Christianity shows a rather persistent and dreary tendency to turn away from that solution, and to be--not anti-human, but beyond the human, prepared to admire the monks and feed the faithful on "fish food."

Dechow: It is interesting that the discussion questions ask about our criteria. I wonder whether we can really make these distinctions clearly in question #1. They seem to involve each other too much and not to be easily separable. For example, what criteria are there for distinguishing between a literal or a metaphorical conception of apocalyptic eschatology? Might there not have been an unconscious tendency toward the metaphorical, even in the ancient period?

Shanzer: Professor Grant's paper has a wonderful collection of stories about food, but they are not kept in context. For example, the Wedding at Cana is compared with the Loaves and Fishes and with the pagan Golden Age visions. But I wonder whether it is necessary to look at every story on its own. Is the Marriage at Cana a feeding story, or is the focus something other than the wine? The Loaves and Fishes miracle is obviously "miraculous" about food, but the Cana miracle is a discreet one, showing Christ in an everyday situation. And the same is true about some of the pagan materials. For example, the visions of the Land of Cockaigne taken from Athenaeus were addressed, in their context, not to the issue of food, but to the issue of slavery--how there was no slavery, no πόνος was needed in the Golden Age: cf. the ready-dyed sheep in the Fourth Bucolic. The stories are cited because of their automation.

Grant: But they may be more the same than they appear. John Chrysostom explains that water always changes into wine by divine action, and all that happens at Cana is that the process is speeded up. So he has made them the same.

Shanzer: The Judeo-Christian traditions always seem to have numbers, but the pagan miracles do not seem so quantitative. Why is there not more cross-fertilization? The only place there seems to be any is in the Lucian passage that Professor Lefkowitz brought up; she thinks that Lucian is explicitly criticizing Christian numbers. However, I think that he is really making fun of a pagan sort of afterlife.

Grant: Numbers appear in the Lives of the saints, but the Dionysiac stories simply say "a lot."

Shanzer: Why is that? Does a number make it more or less believable?

Bokser: My impression is that early rabbinic sources lacked numbers (unless they were essential to the story), and the later sources filled them in on the basis of a Biblical parallel. In the last ten years literary critics have suggested that the lack of specificity in the early stories contributes to taking the story ahistorically and thus to teaching some idea.

Grant: There seems to be a trend of adding names and places as time goes on. The later the story, the more "authentic" names included.

Murgia: Professor Grant's analysis is more concerned with cultural factors that gain acceptance for these miracle stories than with the author's intent in producing them. For example, why Virgil used the images he did in his Fourth Eclogue is not important to him; what is important is why, culturally, the Eclogue was popular. And therefore Professor Grant was not looking at what Mark, for example, was trying to do with the miracle.

Grant: That is correct, and a marvelous out!

Wuellner: Then we are dealing with two kinds of facts: the textual or literary facts, and the historical or social facts.

Grant: They are not exactly the same.

Murgia: In the case of the Marriage at Cana, the first miracle of changing water into wine paralleled the last miracle of changing bread and wine into the body and blood of Christ. The first miracle functions to prove that the last can be done. So as the story was originally intended, you would not say that it functions primarily as a feeding miracle.

Grant: It could have many purposes: one traditional one is that it sanctifies marriage. There are many motifs going on, and I would rather not try to get into the author's mind.

Elliott: On p. 16, Professor Grant's conclusion mentions three things: trust in continued providence, human labor, and organized Christian social welfare. I wonder whether there is a correlation between effective social organization, the waning of apocalyptic mentality, and the "spiritualizing of material hopes." Is there a correlation between apocalyptic visions and economic depressions? Or is there a class distinction, a specific class perspective with regard to these stories of extraordinary abundance? The well-off might read the stories metaphorically, while for the destitute or deprived they might constitute a real, material, hope of divine aid, in contrast to any hope of relief from human powers.[7]

Grant: I do not think it can be worked out that way; there is too little known about prosperity or non-prosperity in antiquity. There was inflation, or debasement of currency, but as far as we know there is no particular relation between that and apocalyptic thinking.

Bokser: There was certainly an economic revival in the fourth through sixth centuries as evidenced by the construction of synagogues and churches. First- and second-century rabbinic circles who did not accept the destruction of the temple did not express their hopes in visionary apocalyptic terms. When they did acknowledge the destruction of the temple, when the temple no longer had

---

[7]On the correlation of economic deprivation and apocalyptic hopes see S. Dickey, "Some Economic and Social Conditions of Asia Minor Affecting the Expansion of Christianity," in *Studies in Early Christianity*, Frank Chamberlain Porter and Benjamin Wisner Bacon FS, ed. Shirley Jackson Case (New York/London: The Century Co., 1928) pp. 393-416.

any social reality, and when the political situation in the third and fourth centuries made them realize that there was no realistic expectation of a better or perfect life, then they employed more visionary motifs. So the correlation may not be entirely economic.

Johnson: We should remember that certain stories--Vergil's Fourth Eclogue, or the Marriage at Cana, or the Feeding of the Five thousand--have considerable influence just because they were so well told. If something is aesthetically well done, it tends to carry off its propaganda better.

Murgia: That may explain why, say, the Fourth Eclogues's Golden Age theme is more well known that someone else's Golden Age theme, but there must be something basic to the story itself that is appealing.

P. Brown: My feeling is that, while lists of criteria look good on a printed agenda, history really is a good Irish stew of multiple factors. I do not know anything about apocalyptic or how it happens, but my instinct is that there is a lot of historical naïveté in much use of apocalyptic as a device for interpreting the ancient world. I do think that it is important to note that it is possible for the comparatively well-to-do to do the dreaming on behalf of the poor, for the simple reason that if you are poor in the Mediterranean world, you are so poor that you do not have time to dream, or to write about it. For example, the concept of liminality works marvelously well when applied to the religious experience of the haves; the haves like to become liminal and identify themselves with what they think the have-nots are like. But it is not so helpful to the have-nots. Women's Studies have shown that in societies with traditional male dominance, liminality is great for the men, and largely irrelevant for the study of women's spirituality. When we wonder whether crises produce apocalyptic, we must remember that 80% of the population lived in a permanent state of crisis from roughly the sixth century B.C.E. to about the sixteenth century C.E. There are no rhythms, though there are some ups and downs among the comfortable. If we rethink this, we must rethink our whole chronology as well as the ethics of such early Christian writers as St. Paul. If ancient thought of the end was not so naive and crude as modern scholars are, then we have a lot of work ahead.

Wuellner: I take it that these crises were ecological and economic as well as political.

Dechow: The issue crystallizes around concreteness. What is concrete about what the ancient sources say about miracles, for them and for me? I cannot answer what is concrete for them on the basis of my experience. From my point of view, even the greats--Plato, Aristotle-- are filled with weird mythology. How could they be gullible enough to accept all that? But these things were plausible in their own culture.

The question for those of us concerned with their message of human hope is, how can we interpret the useful function of apocalyptic? As, say, an escalator of the imagination?

Wuellner: And this should be related to the sociological issue that Professor Brown raised: the hopes of the haves compared to the hopes of the have-nots.

Shanzer: Are there apocalypses that are prompted by natural circumstances?

P. Brown: I think not. The natural world and its productivity would have to be thought of as more cosmically meaningful than in the Jewish or Christian schemes. Perhaps it could happen in sixth-century Zoroastrianism, since ecological failure has a preexisting religious meaning. Also, studies of events like the Black Death show that people were too shocked to think immediately. Two years after the Black Death, a letter containing instructions for the correct type of penitential procession was issued. Two years is enough time to build up morale again. My instinct is that apocalyptic thought might correspond more to times of great anomaly than to times of great distress.

Shanzer: Are we not back to the problem of trying to draw connections between times of famine and dreams of plenty, when we do not seem to have support for that?

P. Brown: My comment on that was probably too univalent. But one should try to get to the meaning of the symbolism from which apocalyptic comes. Perhaps this is how we should make it concrete, in terms of the current meaning of things, from reading inscriptions in public lavatories to reading Plato, on the same day, if possible.

Johnson: Professor Brown mentioned earlier that people who are relatively affluent might dream for other people. I wonder if it might be more accurate to speak of leisure rather than affluence. Even a poor man might have the leisure to do the dreaming, like Amos the shepherd or Epictetus the slave.

P. Brown: That is important.

Elliott: We do have an early Christian apocalypse, the New Testament Apocalypse of John, which contains an explicit reference to famine. In chapter six at the opening of the third of the seven seals, a black horse appears with a rider holding a balance in his hand and a voice announces: "a quart of wheat for a denarius and three quarts of barley for a denarius but do not harm oil and wine!" (6:6). Here is surely a vision of depressed economic conditions. The author of this apocalypse was not of lower class. His exile on the island of Patmos was a form of Roman punishment *(relegatio)* reserved for citizens and those of higher social status. This then could be an example of someone relatively better off speaking on behalf of the poor. (Notice also the judgment upon the merchants, traders, rulers, and wealthy in ch. 18.)

Shanzer: But there are three other horses, too, so I am not sure of the correlation between food disasters and this type of apocalypse. It seems only one factor among many. Have we dated this apocalypse?

Elliott: Even if we date it in the period of Domitian, as most scholars do, we still have the problem of finding out enough economic data about that period to explain why this particular author envisioned this particular economic disaster.

Shanzer: How much is literary tradition, as, for example, taking examples from Hesiod?

Johnson: The best commentary for questions of famine and survival is David Magie's *Roman Rule in Asia Minor*.

Murgia: Professor Brown raised two very good points, one on whether apocalyptic visions arise in times of difficulty or of anomaly, and one on who does the dreaming. On the first, I think that traditional Golden Age themes were sometimes used for political escapism, as in *Eclogue* 4 and Horace *Epode* 16, in a time of civil war. The pagan Golden Age themes, in contrast to the Judeo-Christian tradition, do not contain new miracles invented for specific purposes. They are literary traditions, with each poet working in his own variations. Of course only a rich man would dream of being a shepherd; Marie Antoinette played "shepherd" in the Little Trianon, but real shepherds know better, and would rather be something else. These pastoral images in Golden Age poetry came from people slaving away in the city. So you can tell something about the poet's general view of society, but that is very different from the specific miracle stories, attached to specific individuals, in the Judeo-Christian tradition. It seems that the Gospel writers belonged to the poor class, but one assumes they were the voluntary poor, following Christ's words (given with the Loaves and the Fishes), "Don't worry about food; God will provide." Then that is reinforced by the miraculous catch of fish.

I am interested in the popular myth of miracle. I was once trying to investigate the figure of Aphroditus, apparently a male Aphrodite figure worshipped in Crete. Later, Aphroditus was identified as a hermaphrodite, but the earliest tradition represents him as male. We have a comic fragment that refers to an Aphroditus Tychon. I traced this further, and there is, in the Greek tradition, a Bishop Tychon, and two miracles are connected with him. When he was a child, his father gave him a coin to go buy seed for planting, but he gave the money to a poor person. When his father scolded him, he said, "Look in the granary" --and it was filled to overflowing. As a bishop, he saw people in the vineyards cutting down the old, unproductive vines. He told them to plant one of the vines. So they did, and it kept producing earlier than any other, and always on St. Tychon's Day. Are these stories that some wealthy or leisured person has invented, or have they arisen in the popular tradition? How does this relate to Tychon the fertility god? Tychon's staff can become the bishop's crozier. Did someone do this deliberately, or is there some mechanism to handle the transference--and if so, what is it?

Wuellner: Speaking of the popular tradition, we have not yet considered the role of the magic wand in popular magic when it comes to the multiplication of objects (or vivification of bodies). Christ is shown with a magic wand in a fifth-century carving of the multiplication of food.[8]

---

[8] Thanks to K. Irwin, the carving in question was identified as the "Andrews Diptych," now in the Victoria and Albert Museum, London; it is an ivory from the mid-fifth century, probably from Ravenna. It consists of six scenes, the upper left of which shows the five loaves and two fish held by apostles, with Christ enthroned on the clouds; and the middle right panel shows the wine miracle at Cana with Christ touching the jars with a wand. On the wand's relation to the club of Heracles, see Erwin R. Goodenough, *Jewish Symbols in the Greco-Roman Period* (New York: Bollingen Foundation), vol. 10 (1964) 113. 120-124. 131; on Christ with a wand as an adaptation of the Moses figure with a rod, see *ibid.* vol. 5 (1956) 81; vol. 9 (1964) 160-162; on Moses with rod, see also vol. 1 (1953) 24.29; vol. 10 (1964) 30-33. 68. 105. 127-129; vol. 12 (1965) 170f.

Murgia: In the case of Tychon, there is a statue in Cyprus with a staff in one hand and grain and grapes in the other. This identifies the statue as Tychon, but somehow that iconography gets transferred into a bishop with Christian miracles.

Grant: The shepherd mentioned earlier made me think of the Gospel of John: "The good shepherd lays down his life for his sheep." He most emphatically does not. The story of Jesus has been interpreted in shepherd language, and the real shepherd has been distorted in the telling. I have seen shepherds in Spain beat their sheep with sticks to keep them in line.

Murgia: The Persian king regarded himself as shepherd of his flock--but his understanding of "shepherd" was different from the Christian.

Grant: Often these images and metaphors are quite unrelated to the real situation.

Kolenkow: In a typical apocalyptic presentation, the rich become the poor; they change places, or both become the poor. The wise are silent or are ruled by the foolish.[9] There is a reversal, a change of places. That may speak to the issue of the rich speaking for the poor. Metaphors applied to the reality of the past may be applied to the reality of the future, as that from Psalm 74, where God is pictured as cutting off the heads of Leviathan and feeding them to the people in the desert (LXX). What God has done in the past, he can do in the future, and (besides manna and wine) Leviathan shows up in 2 Baruch. Cf. fish at the time of Moses[10] and in the Markan feeding story.

Grant: And in the Magnificat: "the rich he hath sent empty away."

M. Brown: In at least some apocalyptic literature, there is a judgment on the rich. On p. 19, Peter Brown talks about the persuasive miracles that open up the granaries; this ties in with Jesus' words in Matthew, "When you feed the hungry, you feed me." I wonder if this prophetic note of judgment is also found in the utopian literature, or whether this is a distinction between apocalyptic and utopian literature.

Kolenkow: There is a distinction between the justice theme and the chaos theme. In apocalyptic, there is the intermediate time of chaos, after which there is judgment (though justice may occur as part of an epiphany). To me, the picture in apocalyptic seems less to center on judgement than on change accompanied by great difficulty.

Wright: In the New Testament, the messianic banquet has ties to the apocalyptic banquet on top of the mountain in Isaiah 25. What are the circumstances behind the Isaian apocalypse?

---

[9] II Bar. 48:33, 70; 4,5.

[10] Sifre. Num. sect. 95, cited by E. Goodenough, *Jewish Symbols in the Graeco-Roman Period*, V, p. 36ff.

Leahy: The whole relation of prophecy to apocalyptic is very fruitful. Sometimes it is taken as antithetical, usually with prophecy considered "good" and apocalyptic "bad"--a kind of mistake later Jewish tradition fell into. Bruce Vawter thinks that the prophetic eschatology has been somewhat mythologized in apocalyptic, but it is the same eschatology.[11]

Elliott: There are degrees of difference. The prophets look for restoration and renovation, and getting back to the way things were originally. The apocalypticists have given up hope of anything good to get back to, and so hope for a new age. Apocalyptic is a prophetic critique which has lost all confidence in any kind of improvement.

P. Brown: That critique would work when we are dealing with encounters of the first kind, that is, when something totally strange happens. What interests me are the many constant organizing images, of kingship, for instance, which are not replaced by other images from outer space. There is always the problem of people neglecting the gravitational field around which certain images rotate. We might look at feeding, or guzzling, or drinking, but perhaps this particular body of images is actually in rotation around the concept of kingship. There are known Dionysian themes--grapes, acanthus--pulled out of their Graeco-Roman orbit and into the orbit of royal drinking parties. We must remember that certain phenomena may be satellites rotating around more basic images. On that basis also, Christ's feeding of the Five Thousand is a very peaceable picnic compared with what it might have been. In terms of a "king of kings," he really let his followers down.

Wuellner: Does that not emphasize again that in a hermeneutical discussion it is fruitless to spend too much time looking for the background, the sources, from which something actually or allegedly comes? We should look equally hard for its employment, its pragmatic function, the purpose it is now being used for.

Grant: This should have occurred to me before, but it should be taken in connection with what pagans generally though Christians were up to--one big party, in which they ate children and committed incest. The miraculous but quiet and peaceful party would present the other side.

Dechow: Perhaps Professor Grant is tending toward a concretization, and Professor Brown toward a more metaphorical interpretation. If this is correct, we should eventually go back to Irenaeus and his interpretation of Christianity, which was a crucial point of Professor Grant's paper. In the paper, he raised four issues: apocalyptic eschatology, the analysis of past and present, the relation to possible pagan frameworks, and providential care and the gospel of work (which are mentioned only in the conclusion).

Grant: Since I wrote a book on the subject, it seemed best not to go over it all again.

---

[11] "Apocalyptic: Its Relation to Prophecy," *Catholic Bible Quarterly* 22 (1960) 33-46, esp. p. 44.

Dechow: I was impressed with the questions posed and the data presented, but never found out what the questions mean. Professor Brown's remark about the useful function of apocalyptic (p. 17) seems to imply that the problem will not be settled on the literal level for pagans or Christians, but rather is a hope for the future. On p. 24 he mentions the relationship to monastic intellectualization and *apatheia* and that seems an antithesis to some early views of literal interpretation of miracles. This had more to do with the confrontation with non-being that we find in the origins of Western spiritual tradition.

Leahy: To go back to the "difference" between apocalyptic and prophecy, much of Zechariah, Ezekiel, and Isaiah, for example sounds like apocalyptic. And the Apocalypse of John calls itself an apocalypse but makes use of Old Testament prophetic materials. It is true that the structure of prophecy generally looks forward to development in this world, while apocalyptic looks to a world to come, but even that may not be as absolute as it seems. For example, Amos 1:4 "I will send a fire upon the house of Hazael, and it shall devour the strongholds of Ben-hadad." Is that fire so much different from the apocalyptic fire? There may be more emphasis on the visionary, but there is a real continuity in the eschatology. It is God's working that will be fulfilled.

P. Brown: Turning to my p. 24, it is important that known admirers of Eubegrius speak of Apa Apollo, Apa Coptos, Apa Helle, and Apa Macarius with the utmost admiration as spiritual figures of great importance. So one cannot make a distinction between an intellectual streak and an anti-intellectual one in Egyptian monasticism. My concern is that what is wrong about "Pie in the sky when you die" is that it is not found nowadays. Why was pie taken out of the sky? This was a basic image in that society. When you believe that the earth is surrounded by paradise, your real problem is why this material reality does not impinge on the world as much as it should. Occasionally it does, with good weather and the "smell of paradise." One of the suspicious things about Augustine was that he was smell-blind; he says smells do not tempt him. For others, like Eusebius, smell is a primary sensory analog of the glory of God. We have it upside down. The real world is the more physical, and our world is a shadow-world of broken seasons, crops, and social relations.

Kolenkow: In both Jewish and Christian literature, we are told that angels in heaven do not eat or have sex.[12] So you do not do these things if you are playing angel on earth (as a monk). Only bad angels come down from heaven and do these things. Later monks like Cassian also identified their life as appropriating the life of the poor in this age.[13] The Pythagorean life also often says not to eat, or at least not animal food, and some abstain from sex.

Wright: For the New Testament perspective, there is a dimension of miraculous feeding connected with the Eucharist. This brings up four overlapping signifi-

---

[12] Cf. I Enoch

[13] Cf. the pre-Pachomian rule mentioned in the Bohairic Life of Pachomius 10, 19, where all beyond absolute needs is given to the poor. Cassian I, 10, on Apa Moses and J. Leipoldt, *Schenute von Atripe* (Leipzig 1903), pp. 67-68.

cant themes with roots in the Old Testament: messianic, eschatological, covenantal, and sacrificial feedings. All point to a union between God and the people. These themes are picked up in both the Eucharist and the miraculous feedings.

Grant: They would be more relevant if the Eucharist had continued to be a meal.

Wright: The symbolism does tend to be obscured. In theology, one student suggested that the real test of faith was not whether Jesus was present in the Eucharist, but whether bread was.

Dechow: Professor Brown quotes Origen (p. 24): "In a few remarks, Origen indicates the parting of the ways in Christianity. . . .What was truly disruptive for the church, he felt, was a widespread belief in the physical delight of the millenium: 'Pray to God to save us from such teachers.'" That speaks directly to Professor Grant's quote of Irenaeus and the concretization of the millenium. Irenaeus believed in the literalistic millenium to come, on the basis of Papias and the elders. But in contrast, Origen is questioning the problem of miraculous feedings, and so on. Those who would lead us to a simplistic, literalistic interpretation are on the wrong track.

Grant: In *First Principles* Origen insists that there is not any literal food or drink, and in the very late *Canticles* he says the same. We really have two different world views, both present in the Christian tradition, both called Christian. One says that the kingdom of God will come on earth, and the other says it will not. Origen is very clever, but his experience was very limited, self-limited, and his picture of human destiny is absolutely fantastic. After death, the soul goes to a place on earth, in the East, called Paradise, where it goes to school again. That after all reflects Origen's life, which was spent in schools. (Easton is supposed to have said that life in heaven is a perpetual seminar on the synoptic gospels.) Gradually the soul gets lighter, more and more spirit, and eventually goes up to God. Professor Brown's paper defends the Irenaean view, and I was trying to represent both at the same time.

Dechow: Did Origen really believe Paradise to be somewhere on earth? In many passages he considers it to be in another spiritual universe. The polemics against him in the third and fourth centuries are directed against the latter point.

Grant: It is in the *De principiis*, Book 2, either chapter 10 or chapter 11. I tend to present things in a somewhat mystical way; I do not think in terms such as these on the agenda. By now it is too late to start.

SELECT BIBLIOGRAPHY OF ROBERT M. GRANT

Second-Century Christianity: A Collection of Fragments (London 1946).

The Bible in the Church: A Short History of Interpretation (New York 1948). Revised edition: *A Short History of the Interpretation of the Bible* (New York, London 1963).

Miracle and Natural Law in Graeco-Roman and Early Christian Thought (Amsterdam 1952).

The Sword and the Cross (New York 1955).

The Letter and the Spirit (London, New York 1957).

Gnosticism and Early Christianity (New York, London 1959). Revised edition, 1966.

The Secret Sayings of Jesus (with D. N. Freedman) (Garden City, N.Y. 1960).

Gnosticism: An Anthology (ed. and partly trans.) (London, New York 1961).

The Earliest Lives of Jesus (London, New York 1961).

A Historical Introduction to the New Testament (London, New York 1963). Revised edition, 1972.

The Apostolic Fathers (edited), 6 volumes (New York, 1964-68). Vol. I: Introduction; Vol. II (with H. H. Graham): I-II Clement; Vol. IV: Ignatius of Antioch.

The Formation of the New Testament (London, New York 1965).

A History of Early Christian Literature (revision of E. J. Goodspeed) (Chicago 1966).

The Early Christian Doctrine of God (Charlottesville 1966).

After the New Testament: Studies in Early Christian Literature and Theology (Philadelphia 1967).

Augustus to Constantine: the Thrust of the Christian Movement into the Roman World (New York, London 1971).

Theophilus of Antioch Ad Autolycum: Text and Translation (Oxford 1970).

Early Christianity and Society: Seven Studies (San Francisco 1977).

Eusebius as Church Historian (Oxford 1980).

CENTER FOR HERMENEUTICAL STUDIES

in HELLENISTIC and MODERN CULTURE

2465 LeConte Avenue, Berkeley, CA 94709

Protocols not listed are no longer in print. The others are available at $4.00 each, postpaid (US funds). Standing Order Subscriptions will be billed at 25% discount. Make checks payable to the *Center for Hermeneutical Studies.*

PROTOCOL SERIES of the Colloquies of the Center   ISSN 0098-0900

18. *Longer Mark: Forgery, Interpolation, or Old Tradition?* [73 p.]   LC 76-12558
    Reginald H. Fuller (Alexandria, VA), 7 December 1975.   ISBN 0-89242-017-0
19. *Literary Fashions and the Transmission of Texts in the*   LC 76-26182
    Graeco-Roman World. [51 p.]   ISBN 0-89242-018-9
    George D. Kilpatrick (Oxford), 11 January 1976.
24. *Art as a Hermeneutic of Narrative.* [56 p.]   LC 77- 4346
    John W. Dixon (North Carolina: Chapel Hill), 14 November 1976. ISBN 0-89242-023-5
25. *The Hero Pattern and the Life of Jesus.* [98 p.]   LC 77- 4835
    Alan Dundes (Berkeley), 12 December 1976.   ISBN 0-89242-024-3
28. *Orphism and Bacchic Mysteries: New Evidence and Old Problems*   LC 77-21825
    of Interpretation. [48 p.]   ISBN 0-89242-027-8
    Walter Burkert (Zurich), 13 March 1977.
29. *Philo and the Gnostics on Man and Salvation.* [60 p.]   LC 77-14930
    Birger A. Pearson (Santa Barbara), 17 April 1977.   ISBN 0-89242-028-6
31. *The Commentary Hermeneutically Considered.* [31 p.]   LC 78-16340
    Shepherd, Conley, Brown, Dillon, 11 December 1977.   ISBN 0-89242-030-8
32. *A Textus Receptus Redivivus?* [60 p.]   LC 78-15891
    George D. Kilpatrick (Oxford), 12 March 1978.   ISBN 0-89242-031-6
33. *The Problem of Knowledge in Late Antiquity.* [56 p.]   LC 78-15918
    Raoul Mortley (Macquarie: Sydney, Australia), 21 May 1978.   ISBN 0-89242-032-4
34. *The Philosopher and Society in Late Antiquity.* [41 p.]   LC 80-24136
    Peter R. L. Brown (Berkeley), 3 December 1978.   ISBN 0-89242-033-2
35. *The Role of the Christian Bishop in Ancient Society.* [47 p.]   LC 80-24307
    Henry Chadwick (Oxford), 25 February 1979.   ISBN 0-89242-034-0
36. *Soul and Body in Stoicism.* [40 p.]   LC 80-22935
    Anthony A. Long (Liverpool), 3 June 1979.   ISBN 0-89242-035-9
37. *Self-Definition in Early Christianity.* [38 p.]   LC 80-29301
    Ben F. Meyer (McMaster: Hamilton, Ontario), 6 January 1980.   ISBN 0-89242-036-7
38. *Spenser's Arcadia: The Interrelation of Fiction and History.* [49 p.] LC 80-28303
    Wolfgang Iser (Constance), 13 April 1980.   ISBN 0-89242-037-5
39. *Interpretation, Meta-Interpretation, and Oedipus Tyrannus.* [63 p.] LC 80-28919
    Barrie A. Wilson (York: Downsview, Ontario), 25 May 1980.   ISBN 0-89242-038-3
40. *Greek Knowledge of Jews up to Hecataeus of Abdera.* [48 p.]   LC 81-38463
    Emilio Gabba (Pavia), 7 December 1980.   ISBN 0-89242-039-1
41. *Holy Scripture and Hellenistic Hermeneutics in Alexandrian*   LC 82- 4361
    Christology: The Arian Crisis. [92 p.]   ISBN 0-89242-040-5
    Charles Kannengiesser (Paris: Catholic Institute; Notre Dame),
    6 December 1981.
42. *The Problem of Miraculous Feedings in the Graeco-Roman World.*   LC 82- 9676
    Robert M. Grant (Chicago), 14 March 1982.   ISBN 0-89242-041-3
43. *A Commentary on Virgil's First Eclogue.*
    Wendell Clausen (Harvard), 6 June 1982.   ISBN 0-89242-042-1